HALF WILD

A prayer for a generation of roaming malcontents

Whitney Durmick

HOUSE
PUBLISHING

HEARTS UNLEASHED HOUSE PUBLISHING

Text copyright © 2022 by Whitney Durmick
Cover design by Tracy Sword © 2022 by Whitney Durmick
Interior book design by Susan Harring © 2022 by Whitney Durmick

For information about special discounts for bulk purchases contact:
hearts@heartsunleashed.com

Manufactured in the United States of America
Library of Congress Cataloging-in-Publication Data Durmick, Whitney.

Summary:

Part existential crisis, part road trip, *HALF WILD* is a richly told story of discovery through the lens of a woman navigating work, life, and bad habits in her late twenties.

Taking an uncompromising look at her own self-destructive behavior, Whitney lovingly documents her experience of untangling from the throes of anxiety, addiction, and feeling alone in the world. *HALF WILD* rides shotgun as she traverses questions of autonomy and purpose, and explores her ability to craft her own beautiful life. Her writing is unflinchingly self-aware and relentlessly practical, with a masterful eye for capturing the lushness of life.

If you're looking for a catalyst, this book is it. Prepare to be inspired, delighted, and invited to examine the ways you hold yourself back. This book asks you to tap into your sense of wonder as you let your view of the world be reborn. *HALF WILD* bears compassionate witness to our powerful capacity for healing, growth, and creativity.

ISBN: 978-1-7376063-2-1

[1. Non-fiction. 2. Travel. 3. Personal Growth. 4. Self-Help. 5. Adventure.]

ADVANCE PRAISE FOR *HALF WILD*

"Throughout the novel, I found myself laughing at the humor. Whitney is hilarious, and her writing is a perfect template for bringing light to dark situations. She is also a beautiful writer. Her writing inspired me as an author, as well. The sentences are fluid, gripping, and I found myself excited with every new page. There is nothing critical I can say about this novel. I truly believe her story will help many people find light within their own darkness, with the understanding that they are not alone."

—Alexandra Russell, Author of *The Maze: Her Rude Awakening*

"As someone who struggles with anxiety, perfectionism, and the concepts of home and identity, Whitney's story is painfully familiar. Her prose is lush and evocative, making the resonant moments powerful enough to make you pause re-reading and share clips and phrases with friends and loved ones both. Brava, Whitney, for your courage in putting your heart and more-than-half wild spirit out there for the world. May it reach younger versions of us all who need it so that they might find a way home or a path forward through your stories."

—Clair McLafferty, Author of *Romantic Cocktails*

"Whitney's writing is incredible, amazing, and I can (and have) read it over and over. It's the authenticity and vulnerability that makes it so good, and relatable even if everyone's story of life is different. Looking forward to buying the book."

—Lisa B, Product Strategist, Traveler, Photographer

"These pages hold the dynamic perspectives of a brilliant soul. Prepare for the ride of a lifetime. Whitney so accurately taps into the psychology bred by western society's dysfunction, but she leaves room to inspire readers to transcend the environments that wound them. Her transparency says what we are all feeling, yet aren't yet wild enough to say."

—Marco K, Entrepreneur

"I so deeply related to this book. I was instantly drawn in by the incredible writing and as the narrative unfolded I just kept thinking "me too." The beauty of this writing is in the connection it creates. Reading it, I realized I wasn't alone. Someone else is going through it and putting it into perfect words. That was this book."

—Natalie Holbrook, Development Coach at *Rise with Natalie*

"WOW....what an incredible book. Thank you for bringing me on the journey to sobriety and finding the beauty and strength of you. With every word you helped me feel not so alone in similar struggles both from my past and now. Your personal story of triumph over your fears is an inspiration to women of every age that we have the power and strength to break free from being made to feel less-than."

—Wendy Niemann, Marketing Communications Consultant

For Mom, for Everything.

TABLE OF CONTENTS

The Scream

A little girl with a bowl-shaped haircut rides her bike in a lonesome cul-de-sac. She is dressed in baggy boys' clothes. She is alone and she can't see me watching. She rides to the top of the street and looks out, waiting. Nothing happens. She rides on in expanding circles in the empty blacktop, wearing my favorite LA Dodgers t-shirt. On her cheek I see the little mole my mom liked to call a beauty mark. I feel the sudden urgent need to grab her by the rosy cheeks and tell her that it's okay, that she's okay. I want to take her to ice cream and tell her that she's allowed to want more and that the emptiness she feels won't last forever, unless she wants it to.

I opened my eyes and felt my stomach turning and grinding like a broken washing machine. It whirred and roiled with a whine that howled in my ears, subjective and unheard. I turned my head to look at my therapist. Her gaze was infuriatingly casual, as if I hadn't just hallucinated myself into my own childhood. My body ached, something pulled from deep inside. It clenched so powerfully that organ failure felt like a legitimate possibility. I asked aloud— only half joking—if I was going to expire right there on her couch. "That's not a symptom, girlie," she said confidently, "it's a *feeling*." She must have thought I was some kind of idiot because I was thirty-something, and she felt the need to tell me that feelings were something that you feel.

"Yes, I know that one could *feel feelings*, but not like this, not like, *in your body*." That space was reserved for orgasms and indigestion. I thought I sounded very erudite and intellectual when I explained to her that emotions were simply concepts to be described with words. "The body," I argued, "is for *symptoms*, and anything that deviates from the banality of 'fine, thanks' means something is wrong." And something *was* wrong, because when I saw that lonely little girl on her bike, I felt how badly she ached for more friends and greater adventures. She was sickly and pained from a lack of giggles, and I needed to fix it for her. Even after decades of growing up and being good, she still rode her bike in concentric circles on top of my solar plexus. The weight of her wheels left tread marks on my insides.

In hindsight, I knew what she was looking for at the top of the driveway. It's the same thing I looked for in sleazy bars and conspiracy forums in the dark corners of the internet. She was looking for any proof to validate her growing suspicion that life was more interesting than it seemed. That ache in her belly was a seed of dissatisfaction with the status quo, planted by a spoon-fed belief that happiness was just on the other side of compliance, watered by contempt for the advice that told her that being good was the key to being loved. She learned to please the teachers and follow the rules, hoping that at some point, life would open up and that howling would stop. That ache she felt for connection was only temporarily soothed by good grades and having a nice time at some sterile, school-sanctioned social event.

Later, I used alcohol and punk rock to quell the surge of sadness or channel it into something that made sense, for a while. I knew, underneath it all, I had been trained that those things that make your stomach flip with excitement, and every impulse that says *go, run, play, feel* are not to be trusted. "Be good," was the only way, and it meant not getting too wild or laughing too long at the dinner table because "if milk comes out of your nose again, you'll be cleaning it up, missy."

No one had to scold or remind me because I felt it lingering in the air, a cloying annoyance with exuberance. Elation-induced exhaustion. Admiration would come only as a congratulations for a clean report card or a favorable review from whichever adult I was on the hook to impress. If it meant a feeling of acceptance that soothed that aching howl, I was more than happy to please.

Pleasing severed whatever connection I had to an inner knowing. Others' reactions took precedence over my own felt instincts. Tragically, it wasn't a hostile takeover. It was an inside job. I heard that phone ringing from within and cut the line with my obedient promise to be good because I expected that the goodness would be rightly rewarded with acceptance and the accompanying feelings of stability and order.

Being good called for a lot of doing—doing chores, doing well in school, doing what I needed to check those boxes. I became excellent at doing and at some point when the ringing phone came back online it ripped through me like a tsunami filled with broken glass. By the time I was thirty the hardest thing to do was just to be, to sit still and feel.

By then, after so much doing, I knew I could do anything. I could stand at any edge and leap. I could traverse the weirdness and novelty of the world, experiencing humanity in all of its forms and not only survive, but also learn through the increasingly high-stakes challenges of modern society. In the face of stillness, I collapsed. My ears rang and my heart pounded and my throat clenched and I believed for sure that it was the end, even as one therapist after the next tried convincing me to just breathe. They tried to remind me that these were just feelings: that they just wanted to talk to me.

It took thousands of hours of sitting and breathing and weeping and dying to discover that deep within me, there was a tiny space that seemed to contain the infinite universe. Sometimes it rolled around and felt like hunger. It was like a compass—magnetic and mercurial. It was the force that powered my little feet to pedal my bike to the precipice and look out and wonder what else there was. It was the hunger for more.

Nobody tells us this. If they do, we can't hear them. We don't learn how to listen to that feeling, our inner knowing, because if we knew how it was a call to greatness, and a dinner bell to come feast at the table of our life's purpose, we would all stop going to work and instead spend our whole lives chasing what makes that little space light up like a disco. Those who would keep us sitting stagnant in mediocrity don't understand that this little space is not a neutral zone like a waiting room, but an empty and infinite void that howls for our attention in one way or another until we finally sit up out of our stupor and take note. It's the call to live.

I don't know when I first started hearing the sound of this void that whined and shuddered as the universe poured itself into me. I knew it roared in triumph when I slid into the world, and when I wailed my very first wail to match it. So, when every day from that point forward I was told to hush, go to school, go to work, get a grip, settle down, do the right thing, I was being guided by a firm hand on the shoulder away from what connects me to you and everything else that hums and buzzes with life.

I was conflicted. I had no reason to believe that school, friends, family, and TV would lead me astray. I walked around like an astronaut grasping for a tether in the limitless expanse of space in my failing quest to just go along and be normal. I hushed the howl and dulled it with the acceptable chaos of everyday life and booze, sex, drugs, ice cream, and pithy comedies. Things started to shake. I was stressed. I was sad. I felt alone. I was pedaling my bike endlessly around the cul-de-sac and no one was ever going to come play with me.

The scream got louder and I lumped it in with all the other demands of life that I thought I would get to later when I had the time to pursue whatever passion it might stir up in me. I let it blend into the background like the constant hum of the air conditioner until I could make time for it. Instead, everything broke and forced me to make time. I had no choice but to listen. It grabbed me by the shirt and spat in my face. It bounced around the walls of my skull and made me wonder if I was going fucking crazy. I tried to diagnose this inner scream, this existential uncertainty. I took drugs and escaped into retail and entertainment and busy-ness, but in quiet moments, I heard that wild wail like a coyote at sundown. Too close. It made my skin prickle and my hair stand up and while my brain thought it was signaling death, it wasn't. That was just its backward way of reminding me I was alive and to stifle it was to snuff out the primal howl of desire that propelled my ancestors across oceans on quests for gold and greatness.

It became un-ignorable. It woke me up in the middle of the night to remind me that life was happening while I was busy scrolling Netflix. It growled from somewhere deep and forgotten, buried under decades of conditioning that wanted me to *play it cool*. If I sat with it long enough in a safe space like the couch in therapy, I could hear it switch its pitch into an invitation to reclaim the power I gave away to my bad habits and lowered expectations.

With the humble attention of my reluctant ears, the screaming gave way to quiet guidance and showed me that what I craved was just on the other side of the ways I limited myself in the pursuit of being 'good.'

There I was, in my late twenties, making a desperate plea to my fifth therapist that my good job, my college degree, and my dramaless relationships were all the proof I needed to finally feel okay. And yet, in a low roar like a close ocean, something invited me to break down from the inside out. It pointed me back toward the tools I always had, hanging on the inside of my heart dusty and fossilized from neglect.

Moving through pain wasn't about the job or the proof. My ruby slippers were on my feet all along when I finally listened, trusted, prayed. When I was ready to hear it, this inner scream confronted me with the fury of my own potential and the monstrous possibilities that would emerge if I stepped out of my own way and came home to myself. I held "home" as a romantic ideal. I would know it by its warm-hearted conversations, pot roasts, and golden retrievers. Home in reality was often cold and lonely, even when it was lovely and comfortable.

The scream I heard inside was homesickness. I recognized it as the booming reverberations of the fireworks that God shot off the day I was born. It was a distant ping of the Big Bang broken into billions of pieces and planted like seeds inside each of us. When I listened for the truth instead of for the proof that I was good enough, I finally heard that the screaming was just a cheer-leader urging me back to a life that felt like home, no matter how it looked.

I tried on a thousand homes in an eager and mostly doomed quest to find a place that smelled right, felt right, had the right people, and room for my books. What I never did, until now, was find a home within the echo chamber of the screaming of my heart. When I let it whisper from within, it reminded me of the power it has always been asking me to claim.

I let it crack me open.

High Stakes Road Trip

An infantry of ants marched blackly across the windowsill above the small counter that the hosts of this rental cottage called a kitchen. All of my attempts to quell their progress up to this point had failed. Legion after legion stampeded into my space from the fallen oak outside like a victorious enemy army and I watched them helplessly, my cheek resting on the cool porcelain of the toilet. This was their home, not mine anymore.

The space we shared was a small, squat, wooded cottage on a hillside surrounded by ancient black oaks. From the top of the meadow, you could see miles of rolling farmland below and if you squinted you might see the blue strip in the distance that was the Pacific. Signs on the trails across the property warned about the presence of mountain lions, but the more pressing predators at the moment were the marauding ants, and a sudden, violent bout of food poisoning.

I stood up and wiped a long strand of drool from my chin. I shuffled back to bed, defeated. I couldn't control the flow of ants into my space, the same way I couldn't control how my stomach responded to eating the slice of apple pie that the waitress promised was gluten-free. My taste buds had known better. That pie was a delicious deception and the proof was in the puking.

I sought a deeper meaning in my setback. As a solo traveler out on the road, I was always looking for signs. This had to mean something. Maybe I was being reminded to stay on my toes, viscerally warned by the unseen forces of the universe that when things are going *too well*, danger is often around the corner. The ants signaled the need to watch out for the tiny things that become mightier than their size when they stack up against you. The pie deception showed how receiving human kindness could have devastating results. *I should have known.* There was a reason I traveled alone. Other people made life complicated, messy. I could achieve an equanimous state of beautiful, satisfying aloofness if I followed my intuition and kept to myself. I was being reminded, even punished, that relying too openly on the kindness of strangers was a recipe for disaster. So, my moment of sudden rashy illness made me feel stupid, exposed, tricked. I felt vulnerable, which was not ideal if I intended to succeed on the road alone. If I were to survive this existential obstacle course, I would need to do a better job of watching my own back. Otherwise, I thought, as protective walls went up around me, I was willingly allowing myself to fall victim to people, places, and pie that is lying about being gluten-free.

For several weeks, I sampled at the vibrant sensory buffet of the Southwest, collecting moments of connection in single servings that kept loneliness at bay. The constant movement was comforting. I stayed mobile and avoided the fear of committing to the wrong thing. Heaven forbid I get myself stuck somewhere, where in a month I might be miserable. As a nomad the road kept my mind busy. Knowing where I was going—and that I wouldn't be there long—made me feel free. There was a lightness in the lack of commitment, but I was looking for something.

A heaviness crept in at night. When the world got dark and I had no one nearby to call, I felt a rush of wind in an empty cavern in my chest and chose to believe it was exhilaration, not sadness. Beneath the buoyancy of exploration was a heavy layer of desire. As my odometer ticked up and up, so did the ache I felt to belong somewhere, for once. In Tombstone I watched couples in matching cowboy garb mail postcards. At freeway rest stops I watched families sharing meals. I was out here looking for a feeling, hoping that someday in the near future, around some distant bend, I'd turn my car down a tree-lined boulevard in some quiet town and feel suddenly, undeniably *home*. Then I would know I had reached the end of my road, where I could trade exploration for expansion.

In every town and city I spoke to someone who loved their home so whole-bodily that they opened businesses to share it with people passing through. Their local guidance clued me in to technicolor sunrises and heart-pounding hikes to cactus-ringed crests of crimson rock formations. With help, I found treasures on the road—turquoise rings in sterling settings, a rabbit felt hat, and once a fleeting and rare sense of calm as the sunset from an azure sky lit the adobe walls on fire.

In Santa Fe, I fingered Zuni stone fetishes of animals, set out in bright glass cases to attract the attention of the people who collected Native art or who, like me, sought wisdom in any form they could find it. The woman working in the shop had come to New Mexico when she realized her family would always hold her at arm's length for her wild dreams of animals and hunting for magic rocks in the creek. I picked up a mountain lion carved from labradorite and held it up to the light. I saw that every angle revealed a different shimmer from within while she explained that cougar medicine was about independence and roaming free. The bluish glow and hidden golden streaks reminded me of the Northern Lights. I wondered if I should plan a trip to see them next. I found some Velcro and fastened the mountain lion to my dashboard where it could catch the sunlight and show off the glow behind the heavy swamp-green feldspar.

In a dark and wood-paneled hat shop, the maker in residence let me hang out and try on the merchandise while he shared stories of trout fishing, motorcycle rides, and getting electrocuted by a piece of machinery. For an hour or three of a breezy spring afternoon I lived vicariously through his connection with his home, sensing his pride and letting it feed me for a while. All the locals I met said something similar. They all watched their cities change and the cost of living rise. They all waxed poetic with me about finding the next new wild place. I nodded with $7,000 worth of haberdashery on my head while he told me about a stretch of river that no one knew about yet. He thought about parking a camper out there and disappearing. I understood him, the idea was romantic, but I needed WiFi for my job. I couldn't go feral, at least not yet. He sold me a rabbit felt hat at a discount, maybe just for listening. It kept the sun out of my eyes as I traveled west from Santa Fe.

In Jerome, I heard ghost stories, but the spirits got lost in the sound of a wedding party at the honky-tonk. I ducked into a pawn shop to look for silver. The man behind the counter must have recognized me as the kind of person who was hungry for stories.

"Where you in town from?" He asked the question that he asked a thousand tourists a day, and I answered truthfully, in a way that annoyed me for its ambiguity but also held some pride.

"Nowhere in particular, for now."

"Ah. Yes. I've lived those lives."

He told me about his past lives, and I eyed the sterling and turquoise rings in a tray on the glass counter. He met the woman who was his wife in this life several lifetimes ago, he said. Back then, she was a fierce warrior priestess who looked kindly on his conquering viking in exile. She granted him clemency in her home land, and that was how he knew she was his soulmate. His eyes matched the amber in the jewelry case. With conviction he described how it was her wild spirit that helped him recognize her when they met again at a bar in Prescott. She didn't believe his stories about their lifetimes together, but loved him in her ferocious way just the same. I bought a silver ring from him and he took off forty percent, maybe for listening, maybe because he recognized me as a shipmate from his time on the high seas. He winked and told me I could return the favor in the next life.

I passed into California under an icy white sky with a soundtrack of the freeway roar. My car chewed up the desert swiftly and I began to ascend from the floor of the Anza Borrego just as the sun began to dip behind the mountains. The deepening shadows were a relief after staring into the hypnotizing brightness of the desert sun all afternoon. The higher peaks in the distance held onto the final golden sunbeams as the sky unraveled into the azure and indigo tones of the cool calm ocean that lay a hundred miles beyond. I nosed up switchback roads and rolled my windows down. The air cooled and smelled like sage and sweetgrass.

I was near enough to my day's destination to begin to transition out of road time—that altered state that feels like walking on a travelator at the airport. From Sedona that morning, mile after mile had slid effortlessly under my tires, but now, the moving walkway was nearing its end. I breathed deeply and let my shoulders drop from my ears as I eased the car into an east-facing pullout. From the precipice, I watched the rising full moon shimmer like a gold coin beyond the ocotillos and took stock of the fading day and those that lie ahead.

I stretched and watched a hummingbird hover briefly above the flowering bushes before zooming onto the next and feeling a pang of recognition. I was also flitting flower to flower, collecting stories and stones. Like my labradorite lion, rocks I bought in shops lined my pockets and tumbled out of my cup-holders. I collected them as if their heft could keep me pinned to one place on a map, to weigh down my wandering mind. My next several stops were mapped out with the intention to sample the facets of California, the state where I was born but had fled a decade prior for college and to indulge the contempt I felt for the insane cost of living. I held California in my heart. I loved and related to the dynamism of the landscape and the lushness of the life I lived here. But I left when staying felt irrational. California seemed to believe that the cure for every ill was a tax or an arbitrary rule. The wildness of the state that held mountains, deserts, and oceans pounding jutting cliffs contrasted sharply with the neutered politics and inconvenience of traffic and crowds. Out of spite and frugality I fled for Colorado as soon as I graduated high school. My friends there swooned over the state, counted their blessings to live in a place with so much natural beauty. I understood it at an intellectual level but that irrational part of my heart missed the ocean. I was back to try to feel my way back in. If, after a decade of trying and failing to make other places work, California truly felt like home, I could swallow my pride and fork over the ransom money.

So the first stop was Julian, where I planned to settle in for pie and the small-town scene. I would stay on a farm, and test the feeling of semi-remote ruralness. Then, I was to trade the farm for a condo on the beach, where I would lean into sun and surf and fish tacos. After that, I planned to visit family in Los Angeles, the city of my birth and evoker of a lifetime of curiosity. I planned my escape from LA with a hard pivot into a yurt in the mountains near Malibu where I would stay before passing through the great expanse of Central California and ending up back where I lived as a teenager in the Bay Area. Up north I would visit friends and try on my old home to see if it still fit.

This trip was a roadshow. Each new destination was unknowingly auditioning for the role of my home. That context added extra pressure to every moment. Each sip of diner coffee came with a dollop of discernment—*Could I drink this coffee forever?* In Julian, for a moment, I thought the answer was maybe yes, then disaster struck.

Animal Encounters

A blanket of stars glittered over the rolling farmland. I typed in the gate code to enter the farm where I was staying for the next week. From the listing, I knew to expect an animal menagerie with working dogs and African birds, but at this hour, it was shrouded in darkness. I drove slowly down a skinny gravel road and over a small wooden bridge that crossed a stream that cut through the pasture. A handprinted sign read *Cottage* and pointed me left toward a squat wooden structure nestled among the oaks on the edge of the meadow.

I shut off my engine and let deep silence fill my car. Outside, I stepped into murky blackness. From the woods on the edge of the property a bird screeched a loud welcome. In my periphery I saw a large section of the darkness move. A part of the black night sky was unhinging itself from the heavens and moving toward me. I felt my heart pound and wondered if I would be better off retreating to the freeway and finding the buzzing fluorescent safety of a freeway motel. The hulking black mass loped closer. As the distance between us closed, I smelled musk and hay and discovered that this was not a section of disembodied sky but rather a very large horse. The behemoth approached me slowly and nudged my hands with its nose, apparently quite accustomed to searching newcomers for snacks.

On the cottage's wooden porch, a chalkboard read *Welcome, Whitney!* I used a key from under the mat to open the door and flipped on the lights. The place had windows on all sides which made it look larger than it was, which was just big enough for a bed, a bookcase, and a small breakfast table. The front wall was a kitchenette with enough counter space to slice an apple, plus a sink and a mini fridge. In the fridge a bowl of carrots and watermelon rinds read "for Brownie & Ellen." Now I had names to go with the hulking section of sky that had visited me earlier.

I settled in, feeling enchanted and brave. These were the novel experiences I was looking for. I wanted to be gently pushed out of my comfort zone. I wanted adventure by beautiful means that helped me expand yet wouldn't hurt me. A farm stay in a quaint mountain town was perfect fodder for bragging about my nomad life on Instagram. I slept peacefully, knowing I was in the right place, for now.

I woke to the sound of scratching and a low guttural trill like when someone makes bird sounds by blowing air through two clasped hands. Whatever it was, it was close, maybe right outside the front door. From where I lay in bed, I could see where the pasture sloped upward to reveal the horses grazing and a few shaggy dogs rolling in the long grass. I stood and approached the window slowly, wondering what kind of visitor this animal menagerie offered this time. An egg-shaped cluster of feathers stacked on long, skinny legs blocked the entrance to the porch. A tiny head hung from its serpentine neck and surveyed the dirt under the bushes.

Sure.

While I had not predicted a close encounter with an emu, it was exactly the kind of experience I was out here trying to collect. This moment possessed the pitch-perfect combination of novelty and wackiness, with a gentle level of danger that was exhilarating but not life-threatening. Still, I felt paralyzed by my lack of preparation. Prior to my trips I usually spent days researching routes, scouting out places to stop, and becoming intellectually acquainted with the risks and opportunities that would lie ahead. In no part of my studies had I boned up on the protocol for an early morning emu visit. I didn't know her intentions—was she looking for handouts like the horses or was this a social visit? Did her former lover live in this cottage before it became a rental, and now she visits each morning hoping to find him returned? Was visiting the guests part of her morning routine? Or was she simply enticed by the new smells and the blooming bushes out front? I had two options. I could confront her or wait her out and hope she didn't have plans to linger on my porch long term. Since this road trip, as much as any, was about learning by doing, I chose to lean into bravery. I opened the door and said, "Hello, bird."

Her head traveled up the elevator of her snake neck to consider me with beady, inquisitive eyes. Her feathers bristled slightly, but it felt sensory rather than protective. She appeared nonplussed by my presence, and continued scratching near the bushes. Her occupation with whatever she sought in the dirt was my signal to move forward. I took another step. She stood in the entrance to the porch, blocking my way. To reach my parked car and the luggage I had been too tired to bring in the night before, I needed to pass within a few feet of her feather-covered body. I was aware of the quickness of her movements, that passing too closely or at the wrong angle might break the tenuous agreement our quick eye contact had brokered. I didn't want to spook her, but I couldn't let her spook me either. This was a test of trust.

Were emus more predisposed to fight or flight? As I approached, she stood her ground, aware of me but seeming comfortable in the space she occupied. Fight? She was tall—able to look me in the eye—but couldn't have weighed more than eighty pounds. I figured I could take her, and shuffled quickly past, making it to my car without incident. I took a deep breath and the horses munched grass and looked at me with the same amount of interest that a person waiting at a bus stop watches passing cars. They didn't care, but I was proud of myself. By the time I walked back, my friend had meandered toward the bushes on the far side of the property to reconnect with another, previously unseen emu, this one slightly smaller and with lighter colored feathers. They stood together on a sunny patch of grass, gossiping about the newcomer. If the horses had given them the early scoop, they would now know I had carrots and watermelon to offer. I followed the clear path back to the cottage, feeling slightly scrutinized by my feathery neighbors.

Homeseeking

For a week I sat on that sunny porch, working. I had the kind of job I could do anywhere that had an internet connection, and the kind of boss who was delighted by my travel stories. I turned on my laptop camera during meetings to show the emus chasing each other through the meadow. I sent pictures of the sunset views from my hikes up the mountains to the team chat. So long as I got my work done, nobody cared where I was. That was part of the problem.

I knew what I was doing was cool and exciting by cultural standards. I used my ever-growing cache of travel tales as social currency to prove that I was an interesting person. With full endorsement from work and a society that fetishizes the freedom of travel, I became a hummingbird, all the while wondering if the real brave move would be to pick a place and just stay there. In the shadowy recesses of my mind, there was a quiet wish for some change in circumstances that would force my hand and ground me. In that fantasy, I idealized settling in and devoting my time and finances not to gas and turquoise but to building a community in a place that I loved.

Lurking beneath my domestic fantasy was a roiling layer of fear. My aunts clutched figurative pearls when I told them I was traveling alone, and I understood that for me, the scariest place to go was nowhere. I was afraid that settling down would mean settling for a mediocre life, as if collecting my travel stories and displaying them like peacock feathers was the only validation I could offer that I was a person worthy of love. As long as I had a fresh road story or emu encounter to share, I could shoo away the doubt of my own intrinsic worth.

Don't look at *me*, I thought, listen to *this*.

A life well-lived and tastefully documented was quantifiable proof that I was okay, and proving myself felt like purpose, even when it made me feel restless and manic on an endless search for the *most* best path.

Before any trip, there was a ramp-up period. It started subconsciously, inspired by an exotic snap from Instagram or a billboard with a beach that I passed but didn't consciously notice on the freeway. Then, a churning restlessness in my guts drew my attention to the fact that something was not quite right. Some deep inner voice whispered "time to go." It was a homesickness, with no home to return to to relieve it. Feeling a pull to just 'go,' I would dive into weeks of deep research, scrolling through curated lists of bests.

Best places to live.

Best cities for young professionals.

Most affordable cities that aren't complete shitholes.

The lists and double clicks kept my inner embers of restlessness burning. I formulated the next way I would chase my elusive idea of home, running toward places that were lovely on paper. I believed I could think my way out of feeling stuck and scared and disconnected, as if I could mentally engineer a home for myself. The search was superficial, covering basics like housing prices and school quality, proximity to yoga studios and abundance of hiking trails, but they made me feel accomplished.

I checked arbitrary boxes and let whole afternoons pass, feeling like I was accomplishing something by clicking and double clicking on maps. When it came time to actually do something about it though, the excitement and planning of the trip crowded out any opportunity to sink in and experience the places I had so meticulously chosen. I believed my home was out there already, and my friends, lovers, and favorite restaurants were all sitting and waiting for me to show up. I was out on the road looking for that place and nothing less. With those impossible standards I doomed myself to seek forever.

The Purge

My week with the emus was winding down. I sipped coffee on the wooden porch and felt content in knowing I had survived another excursion and was moving onward to the next. I felt I had adapted well to my glimpse of life on a farm. The animals and I had brokered an agreement of coexistence for the most part, except for that army of black ants crawling unceasingly into the kitchen window from the fallen oak outside to feast on the crumbs I left on the counter. I decided not to let that black stripe mar my otherwise peaceful experience.

On my final morning, I went out to breakfast at a diner in town, which sounds simple enough, but was a big step for me. I was on the tail end of a lifelong battle with my digestive system, which seemed to enjoy metabolizing stress into a thousand tiny knives sliding through my insides. My relationship with food that I did not meticulously prepare was tenuous, and sampling at the buffet of life's unknowns made me feel cranky and terrible.

Years of effortful research and resulting impassioned juice cleanses, detoxes, allergy testing, and elimination diets helped me arrive at the conclusion that I needed to avoid certain things like gluten. This trip was my maiden voyage with the new restrictions in place and I had been playing it ultra safe, sticking to familiar and inoffensive foods because it felt safer than playing Russian roulette with my digestive system with a hundred miles left to drive. Still, it was boring and took some of the magic out of travel.

I was in a place that was known for its pie now, and I had just survived an expansive week living out of my element. I let FOMO get the better of me. Claiming a corner table in the cozy dining room, I asked the waitress if she could accommodate my needs. She was confident that they had a gluten-free offering.

I ordered a slice of pie and a cup of coffee and settled into the space to watch rosy-cheeked locals chit-chat into their coffee mugs. The scene was wholesome and simple like a Norman Rockwell print. I witnessed their weekend rituals play out and overheard their conversations: gripes about freeway construction and raising chickens in coyote country, intel on where the local bobcat had been spotted last, updates that Mike at the co-op was out of ice *again*.

I slipped into their world and began to care deeply for these strangers. From my outsider's vantage point, every couple seemed deeply in love and every family was perfectly happy together, their interactions unabashed displays of friendship and familiarity over fresh muffins.

I wanted it.

And why couldn't I have it? Why couldn't I stay here and make this idyllic life my own?

I fell into that trap set by all-inclusive resorts and holiday towns that want you to believe that you can make your vacation last forever. I was the tanned and happy tourist leaving Bali thinking I'd keep eating dragon fruit for breakfast. I was the exchange student returning from Rome committed to walking everywhere and maintaining my sophisticated and newly-acquired espresso habit.

Maybe it's human nature. We seem to have this natural tendency to try to keep what's good long past its expiration. Sometimes I slip into that grasping desire to squeeze the ever-loving life out of something, to take something good and hold onto it long after it rots and fades to dust. I forget that those good feelings are contingent on so many intangible and irreplaceable factors, that they are often special precisely because they are momentary. In aching to keep the travel magic forever, I do the moment a disservice. This bad habit is like picking a beautiful flower instead of appreciating its perfect intransigence in my life.

But because I didn't have a home to take my travel habits back to, every experience was impermanent, and I lacked the stable roots of a home to ground me in my adventures. Whenever I was tickled by an experience, I grasped for something solid. For a moment as fleeting as the steam rising from my coffee, I decided to stay where I was, forever. And in my delusion, I felt content. My pie arrived and I grinned at the waitress like I knew her. She indulged me. I tucked into the pie and read the paper, pretending. Pretending I lived there, pretending that I didn't taste the wheat flour in the pie crust, pretending that it wasn't entirely too delicious to actually be gluten-free. I figured I'd linger all day, maybe go check out that open house I saw on my way into town, or talk to someone about renting the place above the coffee shop for a while. If I could make this my life for a morning, maybe I could make it work forever.

But it wasn't right. It wasn't mine, and halfway through that pie, my stomach clenched a warning that broke the spell. Years of chronic worry and resultant self-medicating with alcohol had prepared me for this feeling. Like a ghastly fortune teller, I knew that my future held gastrointestinal upheaval.

I leapt into action, packing my belongings that had spread across the table in the now-gone comfort and contentment of five minutes ago. I threw twenty bucks on the table, hoping it would make me look nonchalant and generous and not betray the fact that I was bailing out of the restaurant in a state of sheer digestive panic. I stood to leave and blood rushed to my head. My face burned hot and sweat dripped behind my ears. It was going to be a photo finish.

I choked out a thank you to the waitress. The bell chimed above my head as I pushed the door open and slid out past some sweaty and spandex-clad cyclists coming in after their morning ride. My car was parked right out front. I climbed in and sped out of town through the rural outskirts and up the long winding road that led to my cottage. I felt intensifying activity roiling in my guts, and I looked around, prepared to stop and take care of things in front of God and the grazing cows if I needed to. It didn't quite come to that, but it came close.

I pulled into the farm. It was the home stretch. If I could make it down the gravel road and across the bridge over the stream, I would have done it. But, as I approached the stream, a solitary emu blocked the road. She stared at me once again with those small, beady eyes, inquisitive and now ever-so-slightly mocking. Silently, I pleaded with her to understand my plight and my stomach clenched again and my cottage suddenly seemed a thousand miles away on the other end of the meadow. I inched my car toward her and finally, she understood. She turned and slowly vacated the bridge to let me pass, but not without a frivolous rustle of her jet-black feathers that reminded me I was in her home, not mine.

I parked and frantically fumbled for the house keys and a plastic grocery bag just in case. I sprinted for the door and made it inside and to the bathroom just in time. (The body's sense of timing about these things should not be taken for granted.) My stomach knew I was hurrying and doing my best, and it let me get where I needed to get to to satisfy its needs and minimize humiliation. Just a few incredibly violent moments later, I stabilized enough to look in the mirror. My face was covered in a red, blotchy rash. It extended down my neck and all the way to my waistline. My scalp and lower back itched like crazy, and my whole body burned hot.

I figured it was the pie that had betrayed me, but I couldn't be sure. A million reasons came to mind to explain why I might have gotten sick, ranging from purely physical to wildly mystical.

The (obvious) rogue gluten.

A quick-onset virus.

Bacterial meningitis.

Latent emu allergy.

One too many bites from the billion ants invading the cottage.

Perhaps I was purging that which no longer served my soul.

Or being physically rejected by a town that I tried to make mine when it wasn't the right time.

Maybe spending quality time in nature dredged up old wounds of feeling not good enough that needed to be wrung out from my solar plexus.

Maybe the Pluto retrograde was in conjunction with my natal Saturn.

Or maybe I just barfed because people barf sometimes.

I forwent my usual online search of symptoms, understanding that an inevitably fearsome and terminal internet diagnosis would not serve me in this moment. I needed to vacate the cottage and make my way to the coast. Feebly, I packed and cleaned and double-checked drawers. I splashed cold water on my face on the way out of the door, and felt a sudden pang of nostalgia. In a previous life, before I traveled for fun and to quench my restlessness, I traveled for work. For a while, I traveled a heck of a lot; several weeks every month spent traveling to some new city.

I liked the travel. Packing a smart suitcase and walking through the airport with my laptop over my shoulder made me feel sophisticated. Being needed in various nationwide hubs made me feel important. I leaned into the role of savvy business traveler, swiping my corporate credit card with quiet satisfaction as I enjoyed steak salads and a glass of wine at trendy bistros in the cities I visited. By day, I set myself up in the office and led trainings and made myself available to sales reps and consultants who needed to know my software better to sell it to their customers. I ran office hours and spent the workday brainstorming sales pitches and expansion strategies for major customers. I was good at it, and the trips always started well. They then swung like a pendulum from planning and accomplishment to celebration and destruction. I prepared for my meetings with the intention to do my best. I executed well and took every opportunity to interact with my coworkers and clients, often over dinner and drinks. As soon as I had the end in sight, I got sucked into a tractor beam of celebration, and went looking for my gold star for a job well done at the bottom of a bottle.

After a long week of work, I typically felt accomplished, hungry, and lonely. I coped by bellying up to the bar where smiling bartenders and equally lonely patrons were often eager to commiserate. I liked the performance of sliding my business card across the bar and schmoozing with other business travelers in trendy restaurants and classy hotel lobbies. It was easy to bond over our shared frustrations about corporate life. There were always tropes I could rely on to relate to my new connections, because certain things never change, especially in the technology business.

These sales teams are always selling more than the product can do!

Why can't the Product Dev team keep up with customer expectations?

Why are customer expectations so high, anyway?

I bonded with red-faced regional sales managers in golf shirts bearing the logo of their company. I commiserated with marketing leads struggling to adapt to their company's digital transformation. We connected over our careers, and so, so many cocktails.

Fueled by a few drinks and the trauma bonds of corporate careers, it was easy to be clever and charming, but I would get caught up in the moment and stretch the outer boundaries of my limits, lose sight of consciousness, and take it too far.

With increasing frequency, I ended up in hotel bars and airport bars in cities across the country, and the pendulum swung harder. The clients got bigger, the stakes got higher, the drinks came sooner. As my tolerance ticked up and up, I drank and drank to reach it. I tiptoed on the edge for a brief blissful moment before falling hard, often literally, into the pits of a blackout. Too often, my brain watched what my body was doing and left, went to bed without me, leaving my body to flail and grimace with abandon in cities across the United States. I began getting into an escalating amount of mischief wandering around cities like Chicago and San Francisco, often alone and in varying states of inebriation.

In Chicago, I made the safe and sensible choice to enjoy a dinner of crackers and pub cheese with red wine in my room at the Hard Rock Hotel. Then, the city called, and I wandered out into the darkness. In the morning, I found I had desecrated the David Bowie-themed bathroom with neon orange splatters of regurgitated cheese dip.

In Dallas, I conspired with some sales executives to bribe a bellhop for a bottle of wine after hours. We went back to my room and listened to 2Chainz and racked up a hefty bill of room service pizza.

In New York, I sat alone at a bar at a romantic French place in the Village and sweet-talked the bartender until he closed the place. He let me stick around, and we danced cheek to cheek in the dim light of the empty restaurant. We planned to leave together, but as he locked up, I ran away and hid in a recessed stairway of a garden level apartment. (I never was much of a closer.)

The last night of any trip was always the pinnacle of bad behavior, so the days I traveled home began blurry. I woke up woozy and tried to piece together how I had managed to get back into my hotel room. My whole body loosened when I drank, including my right ankle, thanks to an old softball injury. It routinely rolled as I wobbled down the sidewalks in heels. Waking up involved full-body inspections that usually noted a spinning head, churning stomach, and throbbing ankle bone to signal that at some point the night before, I'd gone down hard. Then, I checked for my phone, wallet, and laptop. If any of those were MIA, I would set to fixing that problem first. Then, I took a shower to make my face feel less numb and discover whatever bruises I had acquired the night before. I squeezed drops into my eyes and drank as much water as I could find to stimulate homeostasis, and headed into the world, smirking at my blurry reflection and pretending not to be in a state of chaos.

I headed straight to the airport, happy to get there a little early so I could salve my wounds at the depressing airport bar, which was my favorite pastime. In an airport, you can drink at nine in the morning and no one bats an eye. You can order a Bloody Mary with a beer back before noon on a Wednesday and it's just travel, baby! Through this loophole in the system of social propriety, I cooled the inner chaos with a tall beer and something deep-fried. The practice held off the reality of an impending hangover. The booze and grease settled my stomach, and often there were other people around that could distract me from the ringing in my ears and the quiet shame in my heart.

I liked to crack jokes and make friends with the bartenders and the businessmen and the brittle housewives that shared the bar with me. The banter and conviviality of shared misery was comforting, and we raised glasses to the shared stress of traveling, bonding under the fluorescent lights like we were being shipped off to war. Drinking together created an instantaneous connection, where we all let our guard down and felt a little less alone.

Once I made it home, I walked to the grocery store for some more easy, cheesy comfort food, picked up a box of wine and settled into my couch to celebrate making it through my self-inflicted rollercoaster once again. In reflection, I am equally repulsed and nostalgic for the struggle. It was almost triumphant, how I made my life so difficult for so many years. I can marvel at the unnecessary difficulty of everyday tasks like maintaining possession of my debit card, and look back on years spent smiling through the chronic stress of living on painful, exhausting repeat.

That morning in the cottage was a snapshot of remembered shame. It was a reminder of how far I had come since I quit drinking alcohol and began traveling toward awareness, not oblivion. Back then, barfing was a natural and often welcomed occurrence. But my life had changed. I thought I had changed. I had extricated myself willfully from my self-inflicted chaos cycle. So, the rogue stomach upset felt like failure, like an unearned return to a sloppy state I had worked hard to leave behind. As I closed the cottage door behind me and bid the emus a final farewell, I thanked myself for getting to a place where I could begin to learn to take care of me. I wasn't running away from loneliness (or consciousness) anymore, but I was still running. At that moment, I wasn't sure what I was running from, or running to.

From

I was on a quest. The purpose was to find a home to cure the wanderlust. I knew the task was impossible and was fine with the endlessness of it, because I would never be stuck. I knew I could travel forever and I would never run out of places to go. I called it a search for home because it sounded virtuous, and part of it was true, but I didn't actually believe the place I was looking for existed. Home was ruined by a childhood spent moving from place to place, learning to adapt and adore newness. I was spoiled by a revolving door of new experiences and endless novelty, and no one place could satisfy me. I had seen too much.

Unless I could find somewhere that smelled like California's night-blooming jasmine with the moral core and fireflies of a midwest summer, with the cultural center of a sophisticated university town and the hospitality of a small southern hamlet, I was never going to find it. I needed fragrant fresh-cut grass and crashing waves and desert sunrises within walking distance of world-class farm-to-table restaurants, oh, and it needed to be affordable for a single professional woman.

It was an impossible task, a paradox locked in delusion, and a holdover from a childhood spent haunted by the looming shadow of a moving truck.

My parents had careers that moved us every few years. It was fun. It molded me into the kind of person who could adapt to almost anything, but it had drawbacks. Most notably, moving so much made it exceedingly difficult to answer simple questions like "Where are you from?"

In fact, that question still makes my whole body clench like a fist. I would rather divulge my thoughts on modern gynecology than flounder in the murkiness of a question with no clear-cut answer, even though I have nothing to hide. I'm not running from a dark past or trying to drum up sympathy for some tragic upbringing. I am not a grown-up feral kid or a former child bride. I was not raised in a suburb of Chernobyl. I just moved around a lot. Kind of like a military brat. But not.

A few years ago I was at a yoga retreat in Bali. We were mountain biking down a volcano, and stopped in a small village to rest and learn a bit about Balinese culture outside of the touristy hubs. While munching on jackfruit on the steps of a family compound, we learned that some Balinese bury the placenta of their newborns in the dirt outside their household temples. As the kids grow up, they say, part of them stays planted in their home turf so they stay connected at a molecular level with their home forever. That's one solution to that unmoored feeling, but my placenta is somewhere under thirty-odd years of medical waste in the foothills east of Los Angeles. If she was ever calling me home, her voice has long since gone quiet.

Anyway, I was born in Los Angeles, but left before I turned three. I can hardly say I was molded and shaped by Southern California, even as I watched palm trees sway in the breeze from the sheepskin-lined comfort of my car seat.

The Southern California stint was followed by frenetic years in Iowa, Wisconsin, Virginia, and Ohio. With those data points in place, perhaps I could make the case for being a Midwesterner.

I returned to California for high school. Northern, this time. They were formative years and I adopted the vernacular and parlance like, hella convincingly.

But I couldn't stay put and bailed out to college in Colorado and stayed there, on and off, for over a decade. But I wouldn't dare say I was *from* Colorado lest the proper locals with the "Native" bumper stickers on their Subarus caught wind that another Cali-born heathen was claiming their state as their own.

It's complex. Politics and perceptions come into play more than you might think if you're one of those enviable people who graduated high school with the same people you met in pre-K. I spend a lot of time thinking about this from a psychological perspective. When people ask you where you're from, they're usually just being nice. Or, they are asking if you're from where they're from because they're trying to establish some baseline vitals for your interaction. They want to know what type of place shaped you into the person you are now, and if your hometown was similar enough to theirs that you might be formed into similar types of people.

Because it requires several minutes of context and explanation, my honest response obnoxiously shifts the focus to me and I get annoyed with myself for taking up so much conversational real estate. The answer should take five seconds or less. Mine is an epic tome of a semi-nomadic childhood. It's awkward. These people who ask the question are nice enough and they deserve a response. They don't know that their inane question opens a creaky chest of moldy treasure that is my geographical backstory. I scramble and deflect, and they shake the ice in their cocktail glasses and stare at me expectantly, starting to wonder what kind of weirdo I am that I still haven't answered the second easiest question you can ask someone at a cocktail party. It's not their fault that they just touched my conversational third rail and I am now short-circuiting and running through quippy responses like "All over!" or "It's a long story."

So when people ask, I usually just suck my teeth and stall, maybe scan the people around me for some inspiration. The askers will stare and shift their weight and raise their eyebrows. When I need to say something to avoid feeling awkward the rest of the week because I acted like a psychopath in the face of a *very* simple question, sometimes, in a pinch, I'll just lie and say, "Here."

I'll nod and look away, ashamed and resolved to come up with something better, something quick and reliable that I can use the way normal people just say "Dayton." And that's why I'm on the road, looking for the place that I can refer to without lying when I just say, "Here." In the meantime, here's the real story.

Growing up was a montage of adaptation, and there was no point to being upset about it. There were plenty of perks. I learned early how to let go of attachments until saying goodbye to even the closest friends felt like flipping a switch in my brain. I got used to the idea of never seeing someone again or never going back to my favorite restaurant for the cheese fries I liked. I learned to hold back long enough in new situations to understand the landscape, and then shift like an octopus to fit in with the new surroundings. Each move made me more adaptable, flexible, and self-sufficient. I learned to find the golden lining in every situation. I collected stories to charm people and convince them I was interesting, even though I never had time to actually let my personality develop because I was too busy changing it to fit the circumstances. I changed everything from my clothes to my hobbies to suit my environment. I was a chameleon, a paper doll, a ghost.

Every few years, a new school gave me the chance to reinvent how I showed up in the world with no strings attached, which few people who never leave their hometowns ever get. Somewhere out there there's a kid in high school still getting called "Puke Boy" for that time he hurled on the field trip to the aquarium. I am gleefully happy that that kind of humiliation stayed wherever I left it.

The first day at a new school was like walking into hyena territory wearing a backpack filled with meat. By the time we moved from suburban Ohio to Northern California I was in seventh grade and prepared. My story was locked down and I was ready with masterfully cheerful hellos and lunch table chit-chat. I knew to speak to the pretty girls with appropriately humble deference. When there were boys around, I added off-color details to my stories to signal to them that I could hang. I wanted to come across like an adventurer traversing the world, casually dropping into middle school to say hello.

I mimicked the regional accents I had picked up and poked playful fun at where I'd been. When people responded positively to my origin stories, I began to embellish them. Six states in thirteen years suddenly wasn't that many, so, to pull focus, I counted not only states but numbers of neighborhoods, apartments, or extended-stay hotels. Six became twelve became twenty-two. I gleefully counted places on my fingers like a clown in a crowd of curious kids, A/B testing my stories for impact.

"You've heard of a military brat?" The mob nodded agreeably and opened their mouths, excited to have a familiar trope to glom onto, but closing as soon as I continued with my kicker, "I'm not that!" That gentle dupe always got a lukewarm laugh.

"I'm like a *corporate* brat. My mom's company moves us around a lot. She's a big deal."

I learned tactics for making friends easily. They were mostly benevolent; like always being the person with gum and extra pencils in my backpack. Even if you're not cool or funny, people will keep you around if you add value. I figured if I could be counted on for minty freshness after lunch period, I was a shoe-in to pass the preteen likability test. I threw cartons of Extra and Orbit into my parents' Costco cart to continue opportunistically freshening the breath of the whole seventh grade.

Other methods were less benign. Nothing bonds people together more effectively than the mutual hatred of a third party. I used this to my advantage by shifting focus to the obvious weirdos in the class, or piling on gossip about the goofball teachers. With an attitude learned from mean girls and honed by the ruthless antagonists in '90s teen movies, I protected myself by singling out others. I'm not proud of this. We all want to be that outlier kid who stands up for the underdog and sees through the cruelty of teenage politics to discover the sweet soul under an acne-scarred face. But no, my upbringing taught me to look after my own survival by avoiding ridicule and swimming with the current, even if that meant being kind of an asshole.

It was dog-eat-dog in those hallways, and I had been raised in the junk-yard. I survived, but missed out on those time-tested bonds between kids who went to kindergarten together and were stuck together their whole lives. I quietly envied that unspoken confidence held by people who are a product of where they are from, although they usually don't even know they have it. It's a sense of knowing. It's a comfort of stillness that I never possessed. It was a belief in the certainty of sameness, when there wasn't a shadow of corporate relocation hovering over your shoulder. There was a piece of their identity that was fixed. For me and my family, it was fluid.

I tried to come up with an easy answer based on what I thought molded me more between my formative years in California and the fact that I bailed for the mountains as soon as I collected my diploma.

Quantifiably, I spent the most years in Colorado, but it never felt like home.

My whole family settled down in Wisconsin, which is where they are from, but not where I'm from.

Calling myself something trendy like a *nomad* is obnoxious and conjures up misleading mental images of backpacking trips and apartments on the beach in Thailand. That wasn't it, either.

Geographically and intellectually, I was homeless.

Careful

I was just a sea monkey swimming in her belly. My mother, a promising young executive, rode her bicycle down a sunburnt hillside somewhere east of Los Angeles. The air was hot and smoggy but the breeze whipped through her brunette curls that were permed to 1986 perfection. Then, the story goes, her front tire slammed into a rut in the trail and we both hurtled over the handlebars into a rocky trailside gulch. She was scraped up and violently reminded of the importance of caution, but otherwise fine. Inside her, the warm darkness sloshed around me and her heart pounded a warning to be careful out there.

She said the accident made her think of the nuns in Catholic school where she grew up in the industrial Midwest. They instilled an existential sense of dread in her, in which her very survival hinged on being good and being good meant being disciplined. To stay alive and righteous in the eyes of the Lord, she learned, one must remain alert or risk a ruler-rapped knuckle—or worse.

Iowa / Loss

It was late September and the California Angels were making a run to clinch a spot in the American League Championship for the West. Dad watched the game while Mom (nine months and a week pregnant) checked her watch.

I was seven days late when I reluctantly emerged, silent, and blue. "What is it?" Mom panted from exertion and Dad craned his neck over the huddle of nurses helping me learn how to breathe. Tense minutes ticked by before I let out my first wail and Dad joined in, "It's a girl!"

It took fewer than three years for them to get sick of the smog and long for space to roam. They packed me in a car seat lined with sheepskin and we migrated east, called by dreams of acreage and idyll in the Midwest. In a placid cul-de-sac in Iowa, I learned to walk by patrolling vast grassy expanses with a shaggy shepherd mix named Roxy. Mom worked days and Dad worked nights. I spent days with a live-in aunt who took me with her when she ran errands and let me sit on her lap while she watched her afternoon soaps.

I remember the morning she left. It was early and where her car was usually parked when the sprinklers sputtered across the lawn, only a dry and empty patch of asphalt remained. I spent the whole day in an oversized wicker basket full of stuffed animals in my closet, crying in the soft confines of their fluffy ears and unblinking eyes.

Mom came home from work and invited me out of the basket to eat. It was dark outside and a stack of generously buttered bread sat in the middle of the dinner table. My throat hurt from crying but they nudged me to eat anyway while they explained that my aunt left because she had her own life to live out there in the world. I hoped she would be careful, and come back soon.

What was so great out there that it was worth getting up before sunrise to go find it? I wondered, and spent the next lonely days listening to rainwater in the sewer, resting my cheek on the warm metal cover of the storm drain and exploring my world, which was enormous. I followed the call to explore it, especially in the early mornings when the house was quiet and I felt like the only person alive. I walked up and down the tree line of the sloped forest at the edge of the yard, looking for the rusty swing set that got blown down the hill during the last big storm. I hopped across the little creek at the bottom of the lawn to watch the neighbor feed the fish in his koi pond. He told me stories like how one time he ate a dog biscuit. He said it wasn't that bad, suggesting I try it sometime. I said I would think about it.

I woke up one morning and pulled the shade to let the sunbeams explode into my room and illuminate the dust and dog hair floating against the pattern of pink hot air balloons on the wallpaper. Outside, the world was empty. A plane buzzed by. The breeze gently rustled the leafy trees.

The only eyes on me were glassy and glued to a white stuffed monkey I had fished out of a bin at TJ Maxx in the Quad Cities and named Jojo. He had long arms and a fat belly and seemed to enjoy watching me with calm disdain. I tucked him under my arm, opened my bedroom door and broke for the stairs, then the front hall. I peered around the wall at the bottom of the stairs, sensing for an adult. Gentle snores floated from my parents' room. Roxy napped under the dining room table. She lifted her head to consider me with soulful brown eyes and darted out the screen door before it slammed shut behind me.

This flyover town was notable for no reason beyond the local ketchup factory. Sometimes the air stunk like vinegar, but not today. Crows cawed hollow from the power lines, breaking the calm as I crossed the blacktop circle and joined the sidewalk on the other side of the street, walking with great intention toward the sandbox in the backyard a few doors up.

When I arrived, I found the sandbox empty. I set Jojo on the edge where he could chaperone as I settled in and assessed the resident child's inventory of faded pastel pails and scoops. The sand was damp on my bare legs and I dug my feet into the coolness, kicking a few grains gently at Roxy, who followed me all the way and was sniffing around in the grass.

I decided to build a new home. I began construction on my sand mansion using buckets to break ground and assemble great piles of sand that I believed would emerge as a princess-worthy castle with the right sequence of pats from my faded pink spade. The first turret was just emerging when a shadow poured over my sandbox kingdom. I squinted into the blocked bright sunshine and saw Dad materialize with arms pumping, huffing like a train as he jogged toward me.

I figured he had come to play, and thought *finally*.

I had achieved an important milestone by successfully occupying myself and playing quietly, out here in the world by myself. I thought my great sand-box adventure proved that I was smart and industrious and by all accounts, a good girl. When I saw Dad's face up close, I wasn't so sure. His eyebrows made an angry V and he reached down and grabbed my arm with hot, sandpaper hands. My feet lifted out of their cool sand caves, and the shift in the foundation brought my whole dream house tumbling down.

I yelled "JoJo!" and pointed at my monkey as I was airlifted away. Dad bent, still breathing heavily, and rescued Jojo from the sandy wreckage of our mansion. I rode home on his back and when we got back he let me slide down to the floor of the patio where my toys were. He turned the corner into the darkened kitchen, and I began sorting my blocks to restart construction. From the kitchen, I heard him sigh and pick up the cream-colored phone on the wall.

"So your daughter decided to just take herself for a walk up the street with her monkey and her dog. No, the REAL dog! I know. I know. Well I was asl… Listen. She's safe now. She's in with her toys on the porch. No, no, we're fine. Right. See you later."

He reappeared and leaned on the doorway, looking down on me with the V still in his eyebrows, but he didn't seem so mad. He looked like he did the time that Roxy had gotten parvovirus and almost died. It made my hands clammy and all of a sudden I wondered if I was in trouble for going out into the world by myself.

Dad turned his back and returned to the dark expanse of the house. I glanced at Jojo, sitting splayed on a sandy tile floor. His shiny black eyes stared back, unfazed.

Wisconsin / Fear

Dad landed a job up north and the family began a cycle of sporadic splintering that became our normal. Dad left to start his new job and took my older brother with him. I stayed back with Mom as she worked on selling the house. This setup lasted months, geologic time in a toddler's mind, and I forgot what Dad looked like. On more than one occasion I ran eagerly up to some man in a grocery store or parking lot, believing he was my father, with my arms spread open, ready to be picked up and squeezed only to discover that I was attempting to embrace a stranger.

When the Iowa house finally sold, we reconvened in an apartment building painted a drab gray that matched the bleak Wisconsin winter sky. I slept on two chairs pushed together. The one-bedroom unit was across the street from a small municipal zoo where my brother and I walked and explored animal exhibits and playground pieces that were modeled after wheels of cheese. We visited bears, buffalo, raccoons, and a moose who emerged from her giant grassland enclosure to follow us along the fence line. We harassed her through the fence, once getting her so worked up that she sneezed and showered us with drool. We wandered endlessly, unsupervised, once getting escorted home by park security after my brother pointed a convincing looking BB gun at the ducks in the pond.

Eventually, we moved into a house shaped like a barn on a street that ran parallel to a dozen other streets just like it, with little houses on flat parcels of mowed lawn with bicycles tipped hastily in shallow ditches by packs of kids. One night, after dinner, we all sat in the dark in the front room. It was quiet, except for the chirping from crickets in the trees that danced through the open windows, and the crackling of tension like spring ice that creaked and threatened to break under your feet.

When Mom said she was going back to work, I felt my small world crash down around me. I crawled onto her stomach to weep into her soft curves. Her body supported me for a while then she stood up and put me to bed. In the morning, she was gone. I learned what it was like to be the last kid at daycare, and how to keep myself entertained with the slim pickings of other kids' toys. At Halloween, I learned the importance of wearing a costume that fit over your snowsuit and for the next two years, I trick-or-treated as the Grim Reaper. I haunted the halls of my elementary school in flowing black robes and fake fingertips with long black nails. With a sickle fashioned from cardboard and tinfoil by Ghost Dad, I stuck out like a fractured bone among the gaggles of Minnie Mouses and fairy princesses.

Virginia / Runaways

I was barely in second grade when Mom sat me on the kitchen counter and told me we were moving again. She had landed a new job in Virginia, and she was taking my brother and moving into a hotel by the school so he could try out for the summer travel baseball team and she could start at her new company. Dad and I stayed behind so he could finish work and I could say goodbye to my class.

This time I was lucid enough to feel sad about it. I cried while they explained why it was a good thing and "a promising change" and Roxy was coming with us, and yes, they did have Nickelodeon in Virginia. I shouldn't be sad, they said, I should stop crying, but they didn't understand that I had just made new friends at Girl Scouts and our preliminary play dates had gone well. Now, they told me I needed to start all over.

One morning before the sun was up, I woke up in my parents' bed to find crowds of men in every room of our house. I watched them take our things and wrap them gently in paper before stuffing them into boxes. Loaded into the truck, our boxes were neat and organized. The order attempted to calm the chaos I felt inside, the swirling uncertainty as I wondered how I'd do it all again with some new batch of kids.

All of my things were stuffed neatly into boxes. If a toy was too big or awkward shaped, I had to decide if it was worth bringing with us or if we should leave it behind. A lot of things got organized out of my life because they wouldn't fit in a box. I figured if only I could be like those neatly stacked boxes in the truck, moving wouldn't be so scary. So, I tucked myself into the backseat of the white minivan with the purple upholstery when Dad and I made the drive south.

Somewhere in the twisty roads of West Virginia, Roxy spoke for both of us by barfing all over the backseat. We pulled over on the mountain pass in a blowing snowstorm and Dad scowled and yanked her from the car and tried to scrub the puke with McDonald's napkins that disintegrated with every wipe. I huddled against the back tire, trying to avoid the splashing slush from the trucks roaring past.

Our new house was a tall stone colonial standing stoic and alone on a cul-de-sac in a new development across the street from a sprawling cemetery. By the time we got there, the sun was out and I had strep throat.

After a few days of rest, I emerged to explore the new house, which sat against a hundred acres of wild forest. Ours was one of the first houses built in a neighborhood that got planned but never funded. Vacant lots of red Virginia clay lined the streets. Behind the house, the yard sloped sharply to a creek and then into thick woods. If you followed the creek long enough, it led to a reservoir and a dirt road and a quarry that must have been abandoned since I never got yelled at for playing in it. I spent most of the summer before third grade navigating that expanse of commonwealth countryside, wandering through the woods, sliding down the gravel pits, or exploring construction sites of the unfinished houses. It was what adventurous kid dreams were made of. But running wild had consequences.

Roxy loved exploring, too. She wandered off like she had done a hundred times before and came back late with antlers and pieces of hide to chew on. She must have found a treasure trove somewhere out there in the woods. One night, she sniffed around the backyard and let the whims of the breeze tempt her back into the woods where her black fur blended in with the underbrush, and it was the last time we saw her.

For weeks I walked to the top of the hill and called her name, because I didn't believe my dad when he said she was gone. Then he called the road crew and they confirmed why she wasn't coming when we called her. I heard the man say, "Black, like a German shepherd? Yeah we picked it up a few days ago…musta been tryin' to get to that doe we picked up that same day."

I still didn't believe it. I rationalized. Roxy didn't look *that* much like a German shepherd, I thought. She was only half. They must have found some other dog, or maybe a black coyote. I deluded myself and held out hope that we would see her running back up the hill, returning from some adventure with burrs and mats in her fur but we wouldn't care because we were just so happy she was home.

I had to keep exploring the forest expanse without her, thinking about how, if what the man on the phone said was true, she was just running toward something that smelled good and then she got blindsided. The thought made me shiver just as the sun dipped behind the clouds and made the woods feel darker. Walking home, I thought about danger. I thought about how Roxy just left one night and went missing, and how I was the only one out standing on the deck yelling her name. I missed her so badly, and I began to wonder if it was my fault. I should have gone outside with her that night instead of letting my dad open the back door and let her go sniff around like he usually did. I should have spent time training her to avoid busy roads. I could have done something to keep her safe. I felt terrible. We had let her run away, and should have done more. Anger rose hotly from my belly and made me feel sick and suddenly the air conditioning in that tall house felt icy cold and I needed to leave. I hauled a hot pink Care Bears suitcase from the back corner of my closet. In sparkly letters spelled out over a rainbow, the suitcase read, "Going to Grandma's."

I was not going to Grandma's, in fact, but I was going to threaten to go so that somebody might invite me to not leave. I thought about Roxy, how she disappeared into the night, and hoped the same wouldn't happen to me.

I wanted to give my family a chance to care enough to save me. I packed an extra t-shirt, a Toni Braxton CD, some books, and a handful of fruit snack pouches, figuring if I needed to take this gambit through the night that would sustain me. I lugged the bag down the hardwood steps, letting it smack each one loudly, to arouse attention and elicit a response. The sound of talk radio poured up from the basement, where my dad was working. I waited for hurried footsteps up the stairs as he heard the racket and decided to check that everything was okay. Nothing. I slammed the front door.

I decided against going into the forest, which was a place for playing and exploring, and today's mission felt more serious. I passed the wooden mailbox that gave me splinters that are still lodged in my fingers, and out of which a hornet had one time flown out and stung me in the neck. "Goodbye forever, evil mailbox."

I crossed the expanse of blacktop in the cul-de-sac where Roxy used to get so worked up that she ran in frantic circles and chased me on my bike, nipping at my ankles. I crossed the main road where we once hit a copperhead snake with our van. I scrambled up the muddy hill on the other side. At the top, I had to push through thorny bushes onto the freshly-mowed lawn of the cemetery, which stretched in front of me for a mile toward the highway beyond. I set my suitcase down and rubbed my hand where the sharp plastic had dug in and formed sore, sweaty creases. The sun beat down through the afternoon haze and my heart pounded in my ears. Suddenly, the logistics of running away felt daunting. I found a shady spot under a tree and sat down to re-assess. It was too hot to run away. Besides, the groundskeeper was on the other side of the cemetery and he might yell at me if he saw me. It was best to stay on the shady side, where I could still see the house and the cul-de-sac below. Plus, I didn't want to cross that highway, out of respect for Roxy's memory.

I unzipped the suitcase and pulled out a few packs of fruit snacks to keep my strength up. I wouldn't run away, but I also couldn't go back yet, even though I kind of wanted to watch TV. It was getting late enough in the afternoon that the good cartoons were about to come on. No, I needed my family to know I was gone, to worry about me, and to put some work in to come find me. I pictured them huddled around a phone, maybe accompanied by a stern police chief, waiting for some kind of word about my whereabouts. I wrote the headlines in my mind: *Brave Girl Travels the World, Misses Dinner.* My mother would be crying, my father, beating himself up about not trying harder to stop me from leaving, my brother beside himself with loss. They would be so happy to see me when I walked in the front door. It was a perfect plan, I thought, and all I had to do was stay here long enough to make them notice.

To kill time, I walked the rows and read gravestones. Most of them belonged to old people with names like Earl and Mabel, which wasn't interesting because Grandmas and Grandpas die all the time, and they had inscriptions that said *Loving Mother.* What could I put on Roxy's gravestone? Perhaps: *Chased Deer to Heaven* or *Murdered by Negligence.* I'd bring her milkbones instead of fake flowers.

I wandered into a squat, square mausoleum, and pressed my sticky hands against the cool marble of the tombs. The afternoon wore on and I wondered if anyone missed me yet, so I went back to the tree where my suitcase was, laid down on the grass, and formed my fists into binoculars to scope out the house. No change. I scanned the cul-de-sac, including the long-vacant lot next to ours where Roxy would run crazy laps when we got her all worked up. I pictured her running at full speed in compact circles, her furry body tilting forty-five degrees into the turns, then I imagined the headlights and the horn of an oncoming truck, and I decided to walk around some more. The groundskeeper's truck was gone, so I walked to the other side and found a whole section of babies and kids who had died. It was more interesting than the Earls and Mabels, but it made my head swim to think about why a baby or a kid ended up buried in the cemetery. I went back to the tree to read.

The sun dipped and the heat broke a little and I heard the distant sound of a garage door opening. Mom was home from work. My heartbeat quickened. Pretty soon, they would be searching the house and the yard calling my name, checking the closets and under the bed. I imagined increasingly tense conversations and phone calls in the kitchen, my mom crying and hitting my dad with a newspaper for letting me run off. It almost made me feel bad about making them worry, but I resisted the urge to go home. I was in too deep. Looking through my hand binoculars again, I waited for them to burst out the front door or for the squad cars and news crews to arrive.

After a while, the door opened and my dad walked to his truck, pulling out of the cul-de-sac toward the highway. He passed below me and I almost waved, but he was looking straight ahead and fiddling with a bag of sunflower seeds in the passenger seat and didn't see me looking down at him from the top of the hill.

Then the front door opened and my mom emerged and walked right toward where I was perched. I suddenly realized how cruel I had been to make her worry. She reached the end of the cul-de-sac, fifty feet from me. She was coming to get me to bring me home, and I would have to apologize for causing so much anguish. She turned down the road toward where a sidewalk led into the cemetery and I could see a Walkman clipped to her waist. She walked down the street and turned up the path, disappearing as she passed through the trees that separated the cemetery from the road and emerged on my side, a hundred yards away, then turned away from me to do the big loop around the grounds. She wasn't coming for me, she was just exercising.

She got smaller and smaller as she walked further away, arms swinging to the beat of Jock Jams '95, then she made the big turn and started back, past the baby graves and toward me. I couldn't take it. I ran up to her and tapped her elbow. She shrieked and pulled her headphones off like she just discovered they were full of bees.

I must have looked scary, covered in red clay and grass stains from being out on my adventure all day. She looked a little scary too; her face red from walking in the heat, sweat dripping from her cropped hair. She kept walking. I walked alongside her and decided it was time to explain myself.

"I've been here all day. I'm sorry!" But she didn't know about any of it. She didn't know that I was mad about Dad letting Roxy run away. She didn't know I had packed a suitcase and planned to leave forever. She didn't know any of it, and I had just snuck up on her during her walk, like a monster.

"Go home," she panted, "Dad's getting dinner."

"I have to get my suitcase." I half-ran to keep up with her, hoping maybe she would walk back to the tree with me so I could tell her about the day and ask about the babies who had died. Instead, she put her headphones back on and kept walking toward the mausoleum to finish her big loop. It was almost dark as I slid with my suitcase down the muddy hill, scraping my legs on the sharp bushes. Walking into the empty house, the air conditioning felt good but gave me goosebumps.

A few weeks later, I found an abandoned school bus in the middle of the woods. The forest was beginning to reclaim it. I pushed aside the spider webs and the weeds and sat inside on the hard vinyl seats and thought about how the bus could be my secret fort. In there, maybe I could be safe from the things that scared me. But then, a spider crawled across my knee and I saw that the school bus was no safer than anywhere else. It wasn't mine. I was just sitting in there, trespassing.

I left the bus and followed the sound of an engine that rumbled under the cacophony of frogs and forest noises to a freshly-mowed clearing. A man on the mower was riding out of sight toward the quarry and his sweaty back disappeared into a red cloud of dust. I walked through the clearing and watched my white shoes turn green in the fresh grass clippings. As I stared downward I stepped over the silver corpses of snakes who had their heads lopped off by the spinning blade. The sun was starting to dip and I retraced my steps past the bus and along the creek, toward the entrance to the woods that led to our yard. I heard something scurrying toward me through the underbrush and I gasped and prepared to sprint home when this tiny white dog leapt out of the leaves and into the trail. He was small and fluffy with curly buttercream fur and he seemed a little unhinged. He ran circles around me and nipped at my ankles, but when I knelt down to pet him he acted like he'd been in the situation before, nuzzled up against my knees, and made moves to lick my face. He was dirty but well-fed. He was someone's.

Through the woods in the direction he ran from, I could see a clearing and a roofline of some short, brown dwelling. I shooed him back to his home and went back to mine, but next time I went to the woods, I stopped by the creek and whistled. And then about every other time, I'd hear the crashing of tiny paws through the underbrush and he'd emerge to hang out with me. Sometimes alone, sometimes carrying his favorite toy, which was an empty two-liter soda bottle. I showed him the quarry and the bus. He chased ankles while I swung from vines. He napped on the rocks by the creek while I dipped my toes in the water.

Sometimes, he followed me home, and I could hear him scratching at the door while we ate dinner or watched TV. I pretended not to hear so I wouldn't have to explain why a dirty little dog was acting like he knew me. I excused myself and ran up to my room, looked out my window, and saw him standing outside with his bottle in his mouth, staring at the front door expectantly. Sometimes, I snuck out to walk him back to the woods.

Mom was raising us Catholic. Around this time was my first confession and in absence of anything more exciting, I asked the priest to forgive me for having a secret dog. Father assigned a few penance prayers, but didn't seem overly concerned.

I only met my secret dog's real owners once before we moved away. They may have been an elderly couple. More likely, they were just backwoods thirty-year-olds painted ancient in my memory. They had a shack on the other side of the quarry. They told me his name was Teddy, and their toothlessness made it sound like Thutty—and they suggested I keep him. I said no, deciding

I liked our relationship just the way it was. I got to have a dog when I was in the woods, and he had a family that could give him all the two-liter bottles he wanted. Besides, my family had a bad track record with runaways.

Ohio / Blood

My brother graduated from high school in Virginia a few years later. He walked across the stage and into our idling car and we drove across state lines again, this time headed for a leafy hamlet outside of Cleveland. It was mid-summer and steamy when we moved in and I spent days exploring the idyllic neighborhood on my bike.

There was a charming green square downtown with a gazebo where they held ice cream socials. I rode by on my bike to scope out the scene, staying far enough away to avoid being noticed. Everyone wore gingham and paisley as if they had called ahead to coordinate, and they sat in organized groups of smiling faces that knew each other. I rode around the perimeter like an orbiting moon; hopeful but isolated by my lack of adhesion to their agreed-upon dress code.

The kids my age were scrubbed and stylish. In contrast, I looked like I was raised in the woods. Unlike the country kids I hung out with in Virginia who wore Tarheel jerseys to church and ran wild with me through the candy aisles at Kiester's, these kids looked like they could have been on TV. When school started in the fall, the contrast became even more clear. The building was a stately and historic-looking brick monstrosity that looked like something out of the kind of Halloween movie where everything starts off beautiful and idyllic and then the town gets ravaged by some psychotic killer who ends up being a disgruntled janitor or the slighted co-chair of the PTA.

I felt instantly ill at ease in the crowded hallways of suburban middle school. My muddy knees and gender-bending bowl cut got me by in the sticks as I embraced hardline tomboyishness. Here, I was confronted with the fact that the confidence I earned by talking to adults would not translate in the gauntlet of pre-teen socialization. I arrived too sure of myself. I was going to be taken down a peg or several after following misguided advice from well-meaning adults to just *be myself*. 'Myself' loved talking to teachers. 'Myself' was a little too into Steven King novels and held too strong opinions about Major League Baseball which could not be backed up because they were summarily stolen from my brother.

This was a time before the internet. This was before you could tap into a universal collective of style and cobble your identity into any inspired combination that spoke to you. Back then, in the template of teen movies, there was essentially a small handful of types of person you could be, and you needed to pick a thing and be that thing, commit to your chosen identity and do it well or risk some kind of ritual shunning. At least, that's what I believed after a long, lonely summer of watching movies and riding my bike on the outskirts of society.

When I attracted attention for the wrong reasons, my survival instincts kicked in and I set to adaptation. I hid my Spice Girls CDs when I found out boy bands were cool, but girl bands, for some arbitrary hallway council-decided reason, were not, spritzed Gap Dream perfume on my wrists, and hoped it wasn't too late.

The Ohio winter descended in a blanket of cold darkness and so did my resentment for this perfect little town full of perfect little families with thin, pretty daughters and sons who wore varsity jackets out to dinner at the Mexican restaurant, which was paradoxically famous for its hamburgers. I decided I hated it there. Everything about it.

I hated the prissiness and the perfection, the conformity, how all the houses looked the same and did the same Christmas decorations that were tasteful and unimaginative. (Each house placed a simple wreath on the front door and a single fake candle in each window of the Colonial facade, to signal that the house was warm and inviting in the same way as every other house on the block.) This town also had an odd penchant for a particular type of porch statuary: a concrete goose that sat on the front step and wore a rotating collection of seasonal outfits. In the winter, if the goose had not been moved inside to avoid the elements, it might be wearing reindeer antlers or be dressed as Mrs. Claus. The porch goose, like the effortful picture perfection of the whole little town, was nauseating.

Winter raged and months of lake effect snow accumulated in black slush piles on the side of the road. My hormones were raging, I didn't have any friends, and everything was miserable. I was always alone, watching movies after school. I watched *Robin Hood: Men in Tights* on VHS every afternoon until the tape warped and I had to switch to *The Wedding Singer*. Sometimes Dad brought me Triscuit nachos or took me to a restaurant called the Winking Lizard to eat chicken wings and watch sports on the big screens. I craved those nights and tried to make excuses to go there, because going to the bar was the only thing that felt fun. It was a warm refuge where I could be around people without the fear of judgment from my peers. I could talk to my dad about our favorite wing flavors (spicy garlic, always) or how the Steelers were doing. I could tap on the glass of the terrarium that held a giant iguana or play a couple of rounds of pinball. At this bar, I felt stimulated and free.

At school, I still hadn't cracked the code. The longer time went on, the more firmly I established myself as a smartass, prone to lashing out. I was afraid of my peers. They seemed to know something I didn't, and I didn't know where I stood, so for safety, I just assumed I was still the outcast on the bike. I kept a distance from people who intimidated me, and never let real relationships form, choosing instead to assume that everyone hated me, or that I hated everyone, or some combination thereof.

Whenever we moved to a new place, Mom always had work and my brother always had sports. They had a built-in community, while I had to fend for myself in the halls of middle school armed with an attitude. I called Mom, hoping for some sympathy, but the receptionist told me she was in a meeting. Dave was off at college in California. I felt alone and I wanted to escape, and I didn't know where to turn, so I let the pain ooze out into a letter that started with "Dear Mama, I need help…" In it, I outlined the evidence to prove that I was fat, annoying, friendless, and possessed no intrinsic worth. I made a strong case for never returning to school, suggesting that it was time to move again, as it was the only way to save me from the brutality of middle school. I left the letter tucked into her briefcase in the front seat of her car for her to find the next morning.

When she returned from work that night, smelling as usual of lipstick, stale coffee, and air conditioning, she kissed Dad and approached me, arm outstretched holding a copy of *Chicken Soup for the Teenage Soul*.

She said, "I hope some of the stories in there make you feel better." I hoped so, too. This, my first self-help book, was her measured and professional approach to supporting my emotional turmoil in a way that made sense in her world of meetings and processes and performance improvement. As a dutiful employee of her family, I diligently consumed story after ham-fisted story of teenage triumph over bullies and hormones, finding them relatable but more upsetting than comforting.

From bad boyfriends to disastrous prom night carelessness, *Chicken Soup* was the kitchen sink of cautionary tales to reiterate what I was beginning to understand at a cellular level: being a person in this world was dangerous. Being a teenager was walking on a live minefield, and the implications now were not just social exile, but also actual death. It validated the toxic teenage belief that the problems we had: homework, drama with friends, softball try-outs—were actually a matter of life and death.

One particularly traumatic chapter shimmered like shattered glass among the rest. Written from the perspective of a teenager dying on the pavement after a car crash, it chronicled the physical pain of dying and also the emotional devastation of letting her family down. The narrator watched the blood drain from her body and said, "I'm so sorry, Mom" and I wept, feeling guilty for wasting my life not being happy. I read it again and again, traumatized and transfixed by the tragedy, which was so much more compelling in its graphic depiction than the chapters about body image and navigating the pitfalls of young love. I heard my voice in the pleading words of the dying narrator. I identified with her deep regret as her blood soaked the pavement. I resonated deeply with her heavily delivered message that the world was not safe and danger lurked everywhere. It wasn't safe *out there*, it reminded me. And now, it also wasn't safe *in here*. Something was percolating.

I packed the book with me on our family trip to Niagara Falls and got my first period in a Mexican restaurant, which was an extra-strength betrayal because Mexican food was my favorite and now it would be forever associated with blood and confusion. I sat in the bathtub at my aunt's house and bemoaned the loss of the convenience of girlhood. I asked my mom if I could just get spayed, like a dog. She shook her head and handed me a pad and went back out to visit with her sister. When I walked back outside, freshly bathed and feeling filthy, they smirked at my situation. Together, they laughed into their wine glasses and shared a knowing look as if to say, "Welcome to hell."

California / Lies

Respite arrived two years later when Mom got the call to move us from Cleveland to Northern California. By the time I walked into the courtyard of my new exotic outdoor school, my adaptation skills were stronger than the sweaty backs of the guys who loaded the moving truck. I was like a poorly trained Pomeranian with a slightly better vocabulary. I was ready for whatever the mean kids could throw at me at the next new school, which was in a gorgeous town in the foothills outside San Francisco. It barely bothered me when, on my first day, a gang of shaggy-haired skater boys walked past me and laughed theatrically in my face. I knew the tactic, they wanted to send the message that I was so ridiculous that they'd make themselves ridiculous just to prove the point. I got it.

I mean, it sucked, but it was nothing compared to the relentlessness of suburban midwest kids with low vitamin D and nothing else to do. Eventually, it subsided. People got curious and wanted to know where I came from. And finally, FINALLY, those skills paid off. I fell in with an actual group of actual teenagers who thought I was cool enough and even kind of funny. Life got good. Girls who hugged each other when they saw each other in the halls sometimes hugged me, too. I had a solid pack of friends and had developed a consistent identity as a witty and kind of mean but high-achieving stoner girl.

By some miracle, we stayed in California until graduation. Well, *we* didn't. I did. Mom took the next gig in Denver and left me at a little apartment near school to finish senior year. Dad split his time between chaperoning me in the dingy rental and playing high-altitude golf at the new country club in Colorado. I spent the year getting high in backseats and coasting on early college admission.

AP English was the only snag in my otherwise cushy senior year schedule. The rest of my school day was spent lording over underclassmen as the Editor-in-Chief of the newspaper or in jerk-off classes like "History of Rock and Roll." English was the final hurdle, and it presented more than just an academic challenge. The teacher was the kind of guy who would break protocol and lead a tai-chi class in the quad. He'd bring bagels to class and ask us to share our favorite music. He was an aging Berkeley hippie and a sweetheart who tapped into the earnestness of his teenage pupils. I hated him for it.

I hated how he would look at me gently when I stood in front of the class and recited the emotional lyrics of a favorite song, feeling hot tears building behind my eyes that betrayed my carefully crafted aloofness. I was not interested in revealing too much, showing signs of vulnerability that might break down the walls of detachment that insulated me from the inevitable humiliation of public school. Those wounds were still sore, and the defensive scar tissue well-established.

For our spring final, we were to select from several prompts and respond in long-form to the ones that spoke to us on a spiritual level. For my first essay, I chose the one that felt like low-hanging fruit, because it asked you to write about your family. It felt easy, because we were very close. The final version was titled "My Family is Better than Yours" and included fifteen-hundred glowing words about how each of us fit together like the diamond cut pieces of a luxury watch. I got an A+ and raving reviews from the teacher, who praised my authenticity and called the piece "hands down some of the best writing" he had read in years. I glowed with pride at his feedback and believed I had truly tapped in and expressed myself. The words felt true when I wrote them. And they were the truth, the same way a bank teller is telling the truth when she tells a hostage negotiator that the robbers are treating her well. "All things considered, the kidnapping is going fine. The torture is mostly psychological and all my limbs are still attached. They shared their pizza crusts with us."

I believed that my family was exceptional, that our jovial relationships and lack of fights demonstrated that we had figured out some secret to getting along that every other family was just too stupid to realize.

We were battle-tested by a constant low hum of chaos perpetuated by moving in, moving out, and moving on. We had no time to fight with one another.

I didn't even fight with my mom as a teenager, because it never occurred to me to argue or push back. It never occurred to her to push back on me, either. She was usually gone, working long hours at the job that had propelled her into legitimate corporate significance at her multinational company. She was laser-focused on providing for our family by providing for her employer, and the latter got all her time and energy.

She had facilitated a corporate merger in San Francisco so successfully that her services were also needed at the Los Angeles office. She split her time, so when she finally made it home, she was depleted. She left it all out on the field. She wanted a glass of wine and some mindless entertainment. On weekends we ran basic errands together, shallowly bonding over blouses at TJ Maxx and filling the grocery cart with ciabatta rolls and Diet Coke.

In her mermaid-green Mercedes in the Costco parking lot, she told me she didn't just love me because I was her daughter. She said she liked me, too. It was a good compliment and I knew it was because she could show me off to her important work friends, touting my strong independence, good grades, and impressive vocabulary from years of reading books that scared me. It was because we didn't fight. We tacitly agreed to skip the whole mother/teenage daughter power struggle rigamarole of fighting and screaming at one another. I barely cared about anything and she was never around. We had nothing to fight about.

And we didn't just not fight. We also had genuine fun together. My dad and I played foosball in the garage and took impromptu road trips to Yosemite when my mom was traveling for work. We commiserated over late dinners in dark chain restaurants like co-conspirators, slurping Diet Cokes and sharing lighthearted tales of the days we spent in our respective trenches.

I was seventeen and had my driver's license, and it finally occurred to her that this was the time when many mothers with teenage daughters decided to establish some kind of system of governance. It was, perhaps, too late. On a warm evening, the Northern California sun shone gold through the kitchen windows. Dad was grilling something outside and the smell of meat and rose-mary wafted into the house. She walked in the door, weighed down by a long week and a heavy laptop bag, as I was on my way out.

"Where are you going, missy?" she said in feigned persnickety momspeak. I told her I was going to go meet some friends at the mall and continued through the door.

"Wait," she called after me. "Why *exactly* are you going to the mall?"

"I don't know. Katie and Jade are going. I don't have any homework. What's the difference?"

"I don't think that's a good idea."

"Why?"

"I just don't."

I explained, logically, how it was actually a pretty good idea. She could relax, spend time with Dad, I'd be out of her hair. She conceded my points but unspoken trepidation pinched her face. She didn't want me *out there*, but she couldn't give me a reason. Even worse, she couldn't just tell me not to go. She was going to make me do the heavy lifting.

I rolled my eyes at this arbitrary détente, resentful of how she could wield the power without the rhetorical prowess. She only had one weapon, and it would render me immobile. She knew I wouldn't leave without her blessing. She knew I would do anything to avoid the post-mortem lecture that I'd get if I left without permission. She used her trump card–guilt.

"Whitney, I finally have time at home and just want to relax, not worry about you, and God knows what you're getting into with your friends at the mall."

We stood at odds in the kitchen until I finally volleyed back with the only harmonious path forward, in which I maintained my autonomy but also smoothed the ruffled feathers. With calm matter-of-factness that I picked up from her and her tales of boardroom triumph, I said, "If you don't want me to go, you could just say no." For a moment she just blinked, then took a deep breath and tried it.

"Okay, Whitney," she enunciated my name like she was reading a tele-prompter in an audition for the role of my mother. "You may *not* go to the mall with your friends tonight."

"How did that feel?" My voice was edged with snark, but I was thankful for a concrete resolution after the stalemate and went back to my room. It was not the first or last time that I had to use her as a physical proxy for self-parenting.

But when I wrote my senior paper, I needed to believe we were excep-tional and could make insane situations not only tolerable but awesome. It was important to me to hold onto our family mythology; my upbringing was an adventure, my family; a tribe. That was the story that I learned to tell others and myself.

My parents adapted to impress their new neighbors and coworkers. They threw dinner parties where I sat at the table and parroted lines from old movies to get the easy admiration from the adults. After everyone left and we washed the dishes and collected wine glasses, I waited impatiently for the reviews to roll in.

Mom would share just how impressed her new friends were by me and my delightful wit. The validation was a quarter in my slot machine. I needed to hear how well-adjusted they believed me to be. Except I wasn't well-adjusted, I was just wearing that outfit. I had figured out early that it was important to be compliant like the dishes that get wrapped in paper and stacked in a cardboard box. After the first couple of moves, I started worrying that if I made any trouble they might just leave me behind in the next one. I became convenient and pleasing like a piece of collapsible furniture that fits nicely into the truck when it's time to go to the next place, which would be just another place that I couldn't honestly call home.

When I was eighteen I went to Berkeley to buy records and got my nose pierced. Mom was on the phone, sounding exhausted and being mad about it, which was annoying because I had told her I was going to do it, she just didn't believe me. That was on her.

"You asked permission. I said no, and you did it anyway. You spent *my* money to pierce your nose." Her voice echoed around the granite kitchen of her cavernous mountain home.

"Who cares?" My question was serious. Why, of all things, should this matter? College was in the bag. I demonstrated to her acquaintances and the college admissions officers and the AP testing board and the National Honor Society that I was a quantifiably good kid. She had any number of ways that she could brag about me and use me as a trophy like her Mercedes or monstrous house. Therefore, her anger at this moment was irrational. I chose to let it fizzle out. If her authority was toothless before, it was even more vacuous now that she was a thousand miles away. I kept the ring in my nose.

I spent the summer between high school and college in her new house in Colorado. All my friends were in California so I occupied myself by crushing diet pills and driving around. At night, I calmed my racing heart by helping myself to heavy vodka pours from her liquor cabinet. I woke up in the morning worried I'd face a lecture at the breakfast table about staying up late watching *Dazed and Confused* and drinking all her booze. The lecture never came.

But when I went to college in Boulder and she found out I was smoking weed, she held an intervention. We all met at a Holiday Inn because they had moved again and had to fly in from Ohio. I sat on a stiff couch while they asked me why I was doing drugs. I didn't have an answer. She put me on probation and mandated I attend drug therapy and submit to weekly urine tests, which felt like overkill because if we just talked like adults I would quit smoking weed and move on with my life anyway.

I wondered why it didn't matter that I was pulling good grades and also working twenty hours a week at an all-natural pet food store. I asked probing questions to establish why this one seemingly insignificant thing posed some degree of existential risk. She didn't want to discuss it. She wanted the behavior to end, like I was an employee who was pilfering dishes from the office cafeteria. She didn't care why I stole the coffee cups, she just wanted the behavior to cease, and she wanted proof of the cessation so she could report up to her chain of command that she had done the needful thing. For proof, I needed to call a phone number every night—the same number parolees get to call—and listen for if my assigned color was chosen to come in for random drug tests the next day. Until I delivered a sufficient number of negative pee tests, she held me at arm's length while I fit myself back into her mold and proved that I was worthy. I was called to grow up not by development, but by deliverables. It was about the appearance and the checking of the boxes. So long as I continued to deliver proof of my worthiness, I could continue to be a member of her family.

It breaks my heart to think of this now, after so many years of therapy and painful work to accept myself and my flaws—*Why didn't I just say screw it and walk away?* I was wholly bolstered by her system of control, and happy to be influenced by it. It felt like an overcorrection to the lack of structure of my childhood, but maybe part of me was happy to at least be getting the attention. To drop out completely would have meant severing ties from the only support system I ever knew, so I submitted to the new conditions, not particularly upset about anything except for how arbitrary they seemed. *Why now? Why this? Was it actually about safety?* No one had seemed to care when I went to parties in the city and woke up to some stranger's hands down my pants. No one cared when I got a flat tire on the pitch-black mountain road to Santa Cruz at midnight. No one certainly cared about the drinking.

I started having a recurring dream in which snakes were everywhere. They slithered up the walls and dangled from the furniture. They fell heavily from the ceiling and slid menacingly toward me. I called soundlessly for help and tried to run, but broke my fingernails as I clawed impotently at the earth. People nearby went about their business or looked down on me with detached pity. During the day, I thought of those snakes and that feeling of helplessness trying to outrun them. They were an ongoing reminder that I was alone in a world that felt full of threats seen and unseen.

Colorado / Attacks

I attended the University of Colorado. It was an enormous school and I was no one of consequence, just like everyone else. I did what worked in high school, sliding under the radar as a chill girl who wouldn't cause trouble. It was about this time frame when the tactic of making myself small and icy cold began to catch up to me.

I clung to reality with white knuckles in the cold light of day, waiting for the next opportunity to escape it. I fell in with people who were also hiding from their own potential—smart kids who liked drugs and hipster music and didn't know how to relate at a deeper level than feeling each other up in an MDMA-fueled massage train.

On a cold winter night my sophomore year, I sat at the counter of a hot dog joint on a busy thoroughfare, waiting for my boyfriend to finish ordering our food. Sausage-scented condensation gathered at the corner of the window, pooling against the early darkness of a midwinter evening. He walked the few steps over from the cashier and sat down, sipping a soda.

"Did you get me a ginger ale?" I looked up at him wearing a pout that was half-serious.

"Shit. No. Sorry."

"That's okay. I didn't ask loudly enough." I shifted my attention back to the street, putting on my show of sadness. I wanted a ginger ale, but it was a stupid thing to care about. Instead, I watched the guys working behind the counter in the reflection in the window. They turned tube steaks on the grill and sang along to Sublime songs crackling through an iPod speaker. I caught the reflection of the guy at the cash register and recognized him from class.

Next to me, my boyfriend sat hunched into a flip phone, an oversized hoodie enveloping his lanky frame. His brow was knit and he bit his lip while he coordinated shady business with his shady friends. As a result of the text messages he was sending, some guys would show up at his house later and conduct transactions in his small, dank bedroom. He was a pillar of the community of dirtbags and sloppy coeds. Powerful like a small-time mob boss. He had the aura of a respected man, someone needed in society, who others looked up to. I enjoyed this, as one of the many perks of dating a dealer.

Knowing him was like having a VIP pass to a party that was exclusive but sort-of underwhelming. He drove a clean sedan while the other guys I knew drove recklessly in loud coupes and beater Jeeps. Our freshman year, he wrangled a key to the freight elevator in the dorm so while everyone else had to climb four, five, and six flights of stairs to get home, I sometimes got to skip the glute-busting concrete steps and hitch a ride with him. He made me feel safe even though he routinely interacted with legitimately dangerous people. His chosen hustle meant he usually had money so we could spend our nights together eating takeout in his apartment, drinking whiskey out of plastic bottles and playing Tiger Woods on his XBox. He liked dogs, bad rap music, and me. At the time, that felt like enough.

I touched the cool glass window and my finger left a dot in the condensation that I extended into a smiley face. Knapsacked college kids passed on the sidewalk outside on their way back to campus. They tucked their chins, adjusted their earbuds, and shouldered their way through the crowds of students who had ditched their backpacks and were on their way back to the bars downtown. The loose, laughing clusters stumbled and shouted in various degrees of pre-gamed intoxication.

"Hey. Here." I jumped and my fingers smeared the face on the window as a hand delivered a full fountain drink over my shoulder and set it on the counter. I spun around with a grin to face the kid from my class.

"Whaaaaaaat?!" I scooped up the wax paper cup and looked up at him in exaggerated gratitude.

"Ginger ale, right?" he asked. I nodded with enthusiasm and took a sip.

"You are seriously *too* good to me." He retreated back to the steamy kitchen and I looked at my boyfriend, who was now looking up with a raised eyebrow toward this kid who had overheard our conversation and made the effort to bring me a free soda.

"What the fuck was that?" he asked, watching as the kid walked back toward the register.

"I know him from one of my Lit classes. That was super nice, right?"

"I guess. Let's hope he didn't spike it."

"Oh, whatever!" The thought landed in my psyche and exploded like a water balloon full of ice water. Just like that, he might as well have spiked it. Fear splashed in my brain and rippled. It wasn't that crazy. We had friends who thought it was funny to dose each other with hallucinogenic drugs and would laugh as the drugs kicked in on the way to class. "You motherfuckers!" the victim would say with a half-angry smirk as he realized his fate, then fumble for a cigarette to calm the ride. I once watched a kid's pupils dilate wildly as our plane took off on a spring break trip to L.A. We stared at each other and shook our heads, wordlessly acknowledging what had happened to him.

Our brats with sauerkraut and spicy pickles showed up in red plastic trays and we ate them with the speed and vigor of people with no concept of heartburn. We dumped our crumpled napkins and hot sauce smeared paper into the trash and stacked the trays on our way out.

He leaned against through the double doors with his back and let cold air pour into the steamy little hot dog stand. I turned to make eye contact with my friend. I wanted one more data point of interaction to see if I could get any clues to his intentions. Was he the kind of guy who would mess with me like that? He was tucked back by the grill, chatting with the cooks. It seemed wholesome and affable enough. I waved and hollered, "See you in class! Thanks again!" before sliding back into the night. The icy cold mountain air wrapped around me as we crossed the parking lot toward the car, though my mouth still burned with hot peppers and spicy ginger ale. By the time I slid into the cold leather seat, I was shivering so violently my head hurt and I couldn't quite catch my breath.

Let's hope he didn't spike it.

I pulled down the visor and flipped open the mirror, squinting into the feeble light. I looked crazy. My hair was messy on purpose and my eyes were wild. I looked at my pupils, wondering if they were dilated. When I snapped the visor shut, the sound was far away.

"Whoa, easy." He reached over and ran his hand against the upholstery of the visor, checking that I hadn't broken anything. He treated his car like a collector's item. I looked at him, taking in his broad features and baby blue eyes. He looked crazy, too. Together, we looked like miscreants. My eyeliner was too thick. His hair was too long. We were mongrels in edgy mall clothes. I suddenly hated us and what we stood for, hated that we went out to eat like we were pretending to be a normal adult couple then drove home to act like wild teenagers. I couldn't place the part of reality where we belonged and it made me feel uneasy, out of sync with the world. My vision swirled.

And I still couldn't catch my breath. The car felt like a morgue. Something with sharp edges slid with a thud from my skull into my gut like a broken elevator full of screaming people. *I'd been too eager to accept that drink,* I thought, *I'd been too nice to that kid. I should have played it cooler.* Now he was probably talking to his friends about how much of a spaz I was. Lit class would be different, now that he knew I was such a dork. He wouldn't sit next to me or ask me if I had gum anymore. My heart pounded in my empty chest, roasting over an open flame of spicy sausage and hot peppers.

"You don't think I really got spiked, do you?" I asked him as I buckled my seatbelt. All I wanted was some reassurance. All I needed to hear was, "Of course not, babe. That's insane. You're good!"

Instead, he said, "If he did, you'll know soon enough," and turned the key in the ignition. The car prowled up the hill toward campus and his place. Tingly static radiated throughout my body and merged with the disorienting rap music pouring slowly like promethazine cough syrup from the car's speakers. The thought of getting drugged brought waves of fear crashing against the inside of my forehead. Everything felt distant. My vision contracted and slipped around.

I replayed the scene in my mind and it began to take on a sickly green glow in the new context of plot and betrayal. That gesture, that offering of a free soda was so kind in the moment. Of course it was actually an act of mean-spirited subterfuge. People weren't just nice, for the sake of it, especially not sort-of-good-looking classmates. *Why would they be nice?* This was almost certainly premeditated. I remembered the tiniest smile on his face as he walked away. It was conspiratorial, not flirty. He wasn't chatting with the cooks about how funny I was in class, he was laughing with them about how he'd just pulled a fast one on some mouthy nerd. I recalled my enthused response, my eagerness to accept the soda and lap it up and felt like such an easy target.

"What if he did spike me with something? What's going to happen?" My voice cracked, frantic and far away. The question went unanswered. It was a foregone conclusion. This was happening. It was my time. I felt terrified and helpless. The cold made my whole body shake. My head pounded. I braced for what I was sure was about to be a wild night of blacking out and hallucinations, thrust upon me by that mean and presumptuous coed druggie who worked at the hot dog stand, because I chose to accept the ginger ale of human kindness.

I worried about what kind of trouble I might get into, unrestrained in a full-dose unintended hallucination. I worried that people might take advantage of me, that I'd be totally out of control. When we got home, I crawled into bed to hide while I let myself plunge into what was coming. *Any minute now,* I thought, watching Seinfeld reruns play soundlessly on a huge TV as he conducted business in the next room. Blood rushed in my ears—whoosh whoosh whoosh. *Here it comes,* I thought, riding another wave that passed through me like low thunder. Then, like the thundering hooves of the cavalry in the distance, I remembered alcohol.

I tumbled out of bed and shuffled on my knees across the dirty carpet, focused on the mini fridge. I found what I was looking for in the freezer; a frosty cold bottle of shitty whiskey that some friend with a fake ID had left behind. I poured myself two shots and took them in quick succession and crawled back into bed. The warmth of the whiskey spread from my belly to my chest and swam up to my brain. I took a deep breath and I could hear the TV again over the roaring of blood in my head. I stared at the screen and relaxed as Elaine leaned back in her chair casually, confidently, and said with her coy smirk "No, I mentioned the bisque."

I didn't hallucinate that night, at least not in the real sense. I did go on a mind-expanding journey, but it was powered by cortisol and adrenaline and full-sugar soda, not LSD or GHB. It was a panic attack. The first of thousands.

Cope

Drinking was a miracle. It solved so many of my problems. I was scared most of the time. Legitimately afraid of illegitimate things—going insane, getting a B, the end of the world. Drinking helped me feel less scared in the moment. When I began to spiral into panic under the sheer weight of it all, drinking redirected my mental energy. As chaotic conclusions presented themselves in my endlessly ruminating mind, alcohol left me feeling numb and easily distracted. When my mind raced, fixated on disaster and humiliation, booze said it was okay to just giggle and watch TV. When life felt like too much, drinking was a socially acceptable method for checking out. I got a temporary break from the raging thoughts and fears and judgments that were produced by my mind.

When everyday existence felt irrationally mundane and dissatisfying, I drank to be comforted by the glowing screen of a football game and the shallow socialization celebrated by our modern instant gratification culture. Growing up unmoored, I didn't have a firm foundation. Try as I might have to grasp something real, everything felt like it could slip through my fingers at any given moment, including reality. I drank to get comfortable with the truth of the impermanence of our existence. I drank to feel okay with the fact that life is quantifiably insane.

When I felt existentially lonely, unseen, and misunderstood, I drank to get closer to other people. Drinking was a fast track to intimacy that bulldozed my own boundaries so I could be comfortable in uncomfortable situations. Social awkwardness evaporated when we came together under the raised arms of a toast. Drinking, I could believe that I was passing as normal, that others could accept me, that I was doing life right. I gaslit myself by pretending that any bad feelings that I had about people at the bar were just further evidence of my own failure. I comforted my distrust by shoving it into a drawer in the back of my mind to be revisited and ignored in the morning.

Alcohol was a bandaid on the bullet wound of an existential crisis. As it wore off and my eyes reopened to the harshness of the reality I left behind, the panic compounded, and the drinking had to continue. As I relied on it to get by, to facilitate interactions, as the underpinning of my hobbies, it could do nothing but escalate.

Fumbling

It was the meanest thing anyone had ever said to me. Under the sordid setting of a sleazy backseat encounter, a man's eyes stared at me, glowing in the ghastly buzzing blue of parking lot floodlights. His face, so recently disentangled from my own, sized me up and swam with confusion in the neon haze.

He said, "I thought you were a nice girl."

My car lost cabin pressure. The steam of the previous moment went cold and dropped down my spine in icy rivulets. Confusion morphed to fury, though I wouldn't show it. From out of nowhere, this glib comment ricocheted like a rogue bullet and had just blown a hole in the feeble foundation of my fabricated identity.

I sat back and re-assessed the situation in the breathy darkness of the backseat of my Toyota. I wondered what I was doing to him at that moment that made me anything other than a "nice girl." I could have sworn, based on all cultural belief systems, that I was being pretty nice. By calling into question my niceness, he seemed to be holding my convictions about what it meant to be a modern woman aloft under the light of scrutiny, and finding them wanting. He pointed out the flaws in my assumptions about what it meant to be a young, single, professional woman.

I thought I was doing it right, but he called me out. In a moment of fumbling cope, I wondered if he was being a misogynist. I hoped maybe I was embodying feminism by hooking up with him in this bar parking lot after too many car bombs at happy hour. In retrospect, I get why he said it, and why he seemed so betrayed, like I had let him down. I also get why, then, I raged against his words like a pit viper thrashing in a cardboard box. I scoffed and called *misogyny!* while I shared these and other war stories over drinks with the girls. *Can you believe it?* I asked. *What a douche!*

The lead up to this encounter was wholesome enough. We courted at work, where I played the role of pert receptionist, and he, the grouchy manager of something or other in the great expanse of the warehouse. I knew he led a ragtag band of misfits who streamed past my desk in day-glo shirts and cargo pants, but he wore black suit pieces from Express and let two full sleeves of tattoos peek out from the cuffs of his oxford, and sometimes brought me Starbucks at my desk.

It was my first job out of college and I took certain parts of it very seriously. My previous jobs were mostly retail, so I only had movies as my reference for what it meant to work in an office. Informed by glitzy scenes of bustling publishing houses in the big city, I considered the first obligation of an office worker to be looking the part. I figured at the very least, if I was terrible at the job, looking good while doing it would broker some empathy from the higher-ups. But I did not work in a midtown high-rise. I worked in a dusty distribution center in a last ditch freeway stop outside a rundown rustbelt city.

Nevertheless, I walked the halls of that warehouse facility in patent leather heels. I was fresh-scrubbed and fit from doing my undergrad in health-conscious Boulder, Colorado, a city that attracted the healthiest and happiest from the nation's upper-crust suburbs. Hiking and health food were basically mandatory, and everyone was as naturally beautiful as those paint-dripping Rocky Mountain sunsets.

When I graduated in the peak of a recession with no job prospects, I figured I was another casualty of the times, and should take whatever I could get. I went to college hoping to be a journalist and came out with a do-nothing liberal arts degree that meant fuckall in a shutdown economy. Since I couldn't afford to stay in Boulder or move back to the San Francisco suburb where I went to high school, I headed to where my parents were outside of Cleveland. Everyone was a stranger, but the rent was free. So, I settled in and got the job at the warehouse while I figured stuff out.

After barely registering in the college town full of pretty young things, I was suddenly an it girl. I drank in the attention from my new coworkers like a dromedary after a trans-Saharan crossing. I felt for the first time what it felt like to be pretty in public. The validation burned clean and hot and turned me into a terrible person, singularly focused on myself and others' reactions to me. Soon, I not only believed but required those compliments. I knew I was on display, and I made every effort to be an exemplary employee, taking on laminating jobs for the ladies in the cafeteria and doing data entry for the customer care team upstairs. I leaned into my new identity of sweet receptionist with the girl-next-door charm, putting on a show for the forklift technicians and machine operators. Under the surface, awareness bubbled, along with deep fear. I wrote in my journal long and self-loathing entries that dripped with the angst and pretentious prose of a failed journalism student:

Opening the floodgates to my narcissism drowns any and all other traits I might possess. The excuse I've cleverly coined is that I am enjoying a reprieve from the intellectual aspect of my life to focus on aesthetics and a life rooted deeply in the physical. I am harnessing a certain beauty that I have discovered in myself but the more I do so, the easier it becomes to see how fleeting it truly is. Twenty-three and already I see the candle flickering. This cannot be all I have. This pursuit is foolish, arbitrary, a sad excuse for a life for someone who is not creative enough, a doppelgänger.

Cloudy refers to the state of the sky outside my window, framed by bony spines of leafless trees, and the function of my brain, critical thoughts dimmed by the lonely combination of alcohol and television. I feel numb. I am drowning melancholy

with minutiae—material substitutes for real experiences. I may appear to be grow-
ing but am slowly, slowly collapsing within myself.

After work, I spent hours in the gym to stay busy and worthy of praise. I fixated on eating right, compiling insane meals like veggie burger patties with a
single sad piece of cheese on some bread product that was marketed as "guilt-
free." Then, once I was satisfied that I had lived a virtuous day by my new and
tenuous pretty girl standards, I indulged in a cheeky glass of something, maybe
a nice German white wine or something classy with a splash of cranberry. You
see, I believed all those ads that show pretty successful women ending their
days laughing into a cocktail.

After a drink or two, those dark thoughts rolled in like a summer storm
and I took to social media to compare myself to my more successful friends. I
turned a critical eye inward and scolded myself for sacrificing my ambition and
intelligence for vanity. I reminded myself that it was pathetic to be squandering
my potential by working some dead-end job in the middle of nowhere, that I
should be doing better, and could have if I'd made better choices, although I
couldn't pinpoint which choices specifically had led me astray.

Fuck it. It's a recession. I was resigned, and let the booze pour and pour. I
was lonely and under-stimulated, and I stayed up late watching movies about
beautiful people doing impressive things in spectacular places. When I wondered why I wasn't doing incredible things too, I just drank more, so I didn't
have to look squarely into the face of the fear that I was wasting a life meant
for adventure.

Inevitably, I woke up the next morning and pulled on a pencil skirt
and color pop cardigan and ate my little English muffin in the car, doing
my makeup at stoplights, and walked into the building with a fresh coat of
confidence.

At some point, we all went out to some shitty trivia night in some shitty
Irish bar in some shitty strip mall, and things escalated. I ended up in the back

of my car, making out with this manager-of-something. Trained by late night TV and questionably feminist magazines, I made the next move. He stopped me. His face was aghast and half-bathed in that icy blue neon when he uttered that phrase that stopped me dead in my tracks.

Now, I can clearly see that he had every reason to believe I was a nice girl. It was *all* I projected behind my desk with my big smile and my helpful ways. I can't blame him for being turned off when I turned out to be the sort of girl that would go to town on him in a parking lot. And to be fair, I wasn't even sure if I was that kind of girl, I was just trying it on for size, navigating modern romance with a map written by rappers and strangers on the internet. Whatever was left of my own internal guidance was muffled under a thick haze of Guinness and whiskey and that ever-present voice that berated me to be nicer, cooler, hotter, better.

I have since retired my drunken floozy jersey and reflected on this moment from the vantage point of relative clarity, trying to identify why one small comment wounded me so deeply. He wasn't some sexist pig, forcing his preconceived notions of what it means to be a woman onto me, he was just expressing legitimate shock that who he assumed was a sweet girl turned out to be kind of easy. He signed up for wholesome and got a carful of wildcats. But in the moment, his comment felt like a scathing indictment. It squeezed lemon juice into a multi-dimensional papercut in my personal identity. He basically called me a liar for misleading him with my bubbly workplace persona. He expressed disappointment that there was more to me than 'a nice girl.' He subtextually communicated that complexity was a turnoff. He labeled me a sexual failure by stopping and questioning my romantic overtures. If I was going for my Vixen license, I had just failed my road test.

And it felt like a yank of a leash, because I had felt sure, in that moment, that what I was doing *was* the nice thing. After reading books, scrolling internet forums, and listening to guy friends, I thought that being nice also meant being "good." And for whatever reason, my behavior wasn't the right kind of *good* enough. It wasn't his fault, though, that he made me feel small, and wrong. He couldn't have known that any other part of me existed, because what I projected at work, where he knew me, was all glitter. He didn't see the gluttony or the gloom.

Masks

The next morning, I felt ashamed. My head pounded and my heart was sad that I came close to closeness and ruined it. It didn't seem like the world wanted my layers and neither did I. I rolled over in bed and stared at my closet and all the fine work clothes hung neatly next to leaning stacks of old vintage tees from when I wasn't pretty enough and had to be quirky instead.

The contrast of shiny new pumps next to scuffed skate shoes was messy and chaotic. Looking at the mismatched rows made my stomach hurt. I wondered who that confusing person actually was. I couldn't pin her down.

I felt around inside for some truth and felt empty. If last night was an indication, it seemed society wanted me to know that the presence of quirkiness, wildness, multifacetedness made the part of me that glittered a lie. If I couldn't keep the mask on forever, I was being disingenuous by wearing it at all. If I wanted to walk among the living, I would need to decide who I was and embody it fully. Multiple layers and unexpected wild parts were undesirable. I needed to pick something, keep it consistent, and keep it cool.

I stared into the vastness between that delightful girl at work who had served me well for a while, and the chaotic reality of who I was inside. I considered the million permutations and decided that I needed to be the best, most unclockable, objectively unobjectionable version of myself. Everything that was not impressive and good had to go. I would need to purge everything that was not the best version of me. The things I hated, like how excited I got sometimes, the bitterness I felt watching TV alone, the sadness when I let myself feel lonely; these were warts I kept under a band-aid. They were a passing sickness, a pest, an unimportant anomaly, something to be ignored until it could be eradicated.

I set to work designing my masks. I gathered intelligence on what kind of person I should be. I tried on personalities like outfits, hoping that one would eventually feel natural, but not worrying if it didn't, because I was happy enough to play dress-up. I took online quizzes to figure out who I should be, what I should do, and how I should act. I continued to use strangers' assessments of me as my guiding light, which backfired because, when you rely on others for truth and validation, anything less than glowing praise feels like failure. I could only distract myself for so long until my nagging inner critic asked "Yeah, but what are you *doing* with your one life?"

I silenced it at every turn in favor of trying to arrive at the best version of myself through trial, error, and the reward of external validation, and I became completely untethered. I shut down my internal compass. I had no true north. The only way to keep from drowning in confusion and self-doubt was to prove, categorically and continuously, that I was worthy.

The need to be unquestionable manifested for some time as healthy habits. I exercised a lot and paid attention to what I ate. I read books and stayed informed on current events. I did yoga, participated in triathlons, and held virtuous beliefs about trendy topics like factory farming. I hoped that doing it all might pass for a fully-formed identity. I believed that by checking these boxes, I would justify my existence.

Ache

Like a naïve and trusting mother to a fiendish progeny, it took me a few years to understand that drinking was stealing from me. And just like that put-upon caretaker, I let it continue to do so even after I realized what was going on. Drinking slinked into my life and stole my peace every time I woke up wondering how I got to my own bed. It sidled into my kitchen and stole my health with every midnight run to Taco Bell. It stole my phone, my keys, my debit card and left them in dive bars or in the pockets of the bathrobe I wore to watch movies and nurse a hangover with boxed wine and Chinese food. After a solid decade of turning a blind eye to these acts of petty larceny, impish and inconsiderate alcohol crossed the line. It stole my sleep.

I've heard it called the 'drinker's dawn.' It's that moment around three or four in the morning when the sugar from the booze metabolizes and brings your body roaring back to life from the slobbery depths of a passout. I began waking up with my heart pounding in a hypoglycemic fit of fear, basking in the icy glow of my laptop which I had left open to stream mindless TV shows and keep myself company. It was a clear warning that I had gone too far.

I felt the grip of disappointment and chided myself for drinking myself into a stupor. I was Dr. Jekyll cleaning up Hyde's mess once again and extra salty about allowing such a stupid and fruitless activity to steal my precious slumber.

I loved sleep. I slept through loud parties and fireworks since way before

I started putting myself to sleep with spirits. Rest was an important vitamin and I felt a strong sense of obligation toward showing up for my sleep. Without it, I was cranky and uncouth. Days after bad nights were inevitably terrible. I walked around cranky and frazzled, haunted by a vague sense of dread, like I had forgotten something. Those eight-plus hours spent with my eyes closed were a welcome break from the constant distraction and stimulus of the waking world. It was a refueling and a portal into another life where I could fly, communicate telepathically, and commune with otherworldly entities. I took that other life—which was always vivid—very seriously. My dreams were grounded but magical, happening in real-life places with just enough of a twist of the surreal to make them interesting and give me something to bring back to boring waking life. When life was mundane, I could let dreams inspire me. It has always been this way. Even my first dreams illustrated templates of my higher potential that I carried with me. In one of the first dreams I remember having, I stood on the windswept edge of our big backyard. From the grassy vantage, I could see for a thousand miles. I heard a roar and looked up to see a hot air balloon descending toward me, firing its torches to maneuver a soft landing on the lawn. The force of its approach lifted my feet off the grass, and the air whooshing from within the balloon propelled me out and over the cliff. I slammed my eyes shut and felt myself fly away from the slope and safety of the grass and out into the wide expanse of nothingness that should have been the forest. I was afraid until I felt myself float peacefully like a falling leaf. I landed softly on the ground and gently woke up, the exhilaration of flight still pulsing in my limbs. I felt a sweet spreading calm, too, knowing I was protected. I heard a whisper in the whooshing wind that I could fly anytime I wanted.

In another, I was hiding inside a circular clothing rack in a department store. The context of the dream was some child-on-child gang war. A menacing group of children were at that moment prowling the store looking for me, and I was the coolest and toughest version of myself, rocking a distressed denim vest and red bandana that elicited 80's movie tough kids. I looked like an Outsider from S.E. Hinton's novel.

When the other kids found me and tried to roust me from my rounder I said, with perfect nonchalance "I'm outta here," and turned on my heel to escape through the automatic doors of the Burlington Coat Factory. I exhibited a backbone that I never had in waking life. I chased that toughness, aspired to it fruitlessly. The pursuit of that coolness made me seek comfort in drinking. *Drinking was cool, wasn't it?* If I drank, I was cool, like that cool girl in my dream.

After that, sleep was an opportunity to return to a place where I could leap from a precipice and find my way to safety, and I was always eager to close my eyes and drift into that world.

It never stopped being funny that I could wake up and enjoy a bowl of cereal, casual as ever, as if I hadn't just hallucinated myself into a different dimension that suspended the laws of space and time. In comparison, the cereal and the school bus in real life felt dull.

Dreams were weird and mysterious. I craved the adventure of side-stepping reality in favor of the symbolic unconscious. So, I found it wholly unacceptable when drinking continued to interrupt my ability to peacefully transition into my other life. When booze held me hostage on this side, shaking and stressed, I knew we had reached the end of our time together.

Ruin

Drinking ruined my life, but not in the way you think.

I like to think I wouldn't have done it so much if there wasn't some tangible utility. I didn't plan on becoming a stumbling mess. It started with good enough intentions. It was comforting in weird social situations. It mellowed out a loud inner critic. It hushed raging panic. Drinking dulled the voice in my head that made me feel like an outsider. It made me feel normal. It made me think I was fitting in, pulling off whatever manufactured persona could be shoehorned into the scenario to garner acceptance. And there was momentary joy in drinking. It was a thing to do that beat boredom. It was a path out of the discomfort of feeling like there was more to life than trivia nights and conference calls. I got excited about drinking and sought out events at bars and breweries where I knew drinking would be the primary activity. I unwound from work with a drink, celebrated promotions and drank away the stress of the week. I paired my home-cooked meals with tasteful selections of wine and bourbon, treating myself to a classy adult dinner before the drinks took hold and I said screw it and tucked into the boxed wine in the fridge.

It never occurred to me that the voice that told me I was uncomfortable might have a point, or that being uncomfortable was a signal and that I could do anything else about it. I guess I believed I was stuck and had to just grin and bear whatever situation unfolded around me. I never thought to wonder why I felt that way or to consider other social situations to see if they all made me feel like I was wearing someone else's skin, and it was two sizes too small.

Had I listened, I may have discovered that I was uncomfortable because I was surrounded by the wrong people, in the wrong place, doing things that I didn't want to do. Had I been brave enough to inquire, I might have spared myself years of blood sugar spikes and the embarrassing entanglements of binge drinking.

But that wasn't the path for me, because I believed strongly that what I was doing was right and normal. So, if it wasn't working, I assumed that the problem was me. The world reassured me at every turn that drinking a lot was a standard behavior for a person of my demographic.

Hang out with your friends, it said, *take a load off, you deserve it!*

Celebrate, have a drink!

Tough day at work? Raise a glass to another week at the grind.

It all felt hollow. Encounters with others felt increasingly fraught and problematic. But I never tried a different direction, I just tried harder, because I had myself convinced. When it wasn't working, it just reinforced my belief that there must be something wrong with me. It wasn't my behavior, it was something fundamentally amiss with my body or my mind that needed to be fixed like a mechanic fixes a leaky gasket.

I was physically sick or mentally ill, or maybe just a bad person, because it seemed like I was doing what everyone else was doing and it was working for them and not for me. I must have had a panic disorder or hypoglycemia or a burgeoning case of some rare auto-immune disorder that caused stomach aches in the face of challenging situations. I gripped that belief so tightly that it almost broke my wrists. It offered the comfort of distraction while I Googled my symptoms and sought out professionals who told me one after the other that I was actually probably fine.

But I didn't feel fine, and so I overdid it, because that's what happens when you try to fill a void with a volatile substance. After a few too many attempts to thrive in an inhospitable environment, the room darkened, my words slurred, my chariot turned back into a pumpkin and I crash landed into a mud puddle of my own squashed delusions. Meanwhile, things escalated and I became less and less fine.

Somewhere in the Darkness

Somewhere in the darkness, my phone rang. I didn't hear it at first because I had just about drowned myself in a puddle of sleepy drool and had yet to come back to the surface from deep within my subconscious. On the third or fourth ring, I began to claw back from the depths and groggily reenter the hotel room. The ringing in the room stopped, replaced instantly with loud ringing in my ears.

My head was thick and I was aware of a throbbing in my knee and the cool sheets were stuck to my leg with something sticky. The red digital letters of the hotel alarm clock said it was 10am. On the other side of the blackout curtains sat Minneapolis, drenched in dreary January gray.

I rolled over. The sheets peeled away from my leg and I noticed the gash and its smear of blood and dirt. I set my feet on the carpet and found my pants, heaped haphazardly on the floor and caked in the same troubling melange. I dug through their pockets and found the phone.

I missed a call from my friend Patti. I didn't know why she had called. She was back in Colorado, we hadn't spoken in weeks, since I had been traveling so much for work. She was the kind of friend that was understanding when I dropped off the face of the planet. For better or worse, she was always still happy to see me when I emerged from a long trip or self-imposed isolation spent hiding in my apartment watching Parks & Rec on repeat with my dog and a bottle of bourbon.

I owed her a call back. It would assuage my guilt of being a bad friend, the kind who was so hung up on my own life that I easily lost touch with others. I didn't burn bridges so much as I let them fall into disrepair and then avoided them out of an abundance of caution. But Patti and I had lived together in college, and we stayed in touch. We had enough shared experiences to bond us more deeply than simple friends from class or Friday-night drinking buddies. We dated in the same circles. We rode our bikes through the back alleys of Boulder after whiskey-drenched karaoke nights. She liked to use my dog as a handkerchief when she cried, draping her body over his mound of thick white fur and sobbing bodily. He was supportive and present while I often sat at a distance, wide-eyed and nervous. She was an early role model of emotional expression, but at the time, I found it frightening and was all too eager to let the dog do the work. I was out of my depth in the face of strong emotions. And Patti—an art student, Pisces, and sweetheart—had all of them.

I called her back, holding the phone to my ear as I collapsed back on the sheets that were streaked with blood from the knee wound. My head pounded and I couldn't remember getting back to the hotel room. I thumbed through the receipts in the pocket of my drenched coat. A bar tab. Dinner and drinks. Another bar tab, plus a dessert order. Through the fog a memory emerged of sitting at the bar in the lobby. It was wholesome and wise like my intentions at 5 o'clock, and didn't explain the blood.

"Hey!" Patti answered excitedly. "How are you?" The question was loaded. She asked like she already knew the answer.

"I'm okay. I'm in Minneapolis for work."

"Uh. Yeah, I know! Do you remember talking to me last night?"

I didn't. Not that it was the first time that I had been physically but not mentally present for a phone call or other interaction with her. Patti and I had spent enough time during and after college philosophizing over too many bottles of her rich uncle's good red wine or whiskey gingers at the bar, that she knew my permutations. And she sounded alarmed.

Which was alarming. I let the line sit silent, in shame and sheer confusion. Usually I was better than this, and could cobble at least part of a timeline together. I didn't often forget getting myself home. She broke the silence.

"Girl! I called you! You told me you were with some people and things were getting really weird. You told me you felt uncomfortable and weren't sure what you were going to do, but that you wanted to bail. You didn't sound like you."

I looked at the mud-caked jeans and my equally filthy coat draped over the desk chair. My eyes scanned to the contents of my purse strewn wildly across my desk and my wallet gaping open emptily. I stood up to look at the evidence more closely, and winced on a throbbing, freshly-sprained ankle. It was the same ankle that routinely rolled when I went out drinking and my wobbly gait sent my weight careening like a pendulum too far out over the sides of my ankles and the tendons couldn't hold the sway. My mud-caked high heels sat by the door, complicit in the injury.

Ankle pain and a blurry mind weren't new, but mud-caked clothing and an empty wallet in a weird city (with the context of Patti's words) were troubling. I tried to use drinker's forensics to put it all together. I had gone out somewhere, with people, and felt uncomfortable.

I remembered for sure going out for innocent after-work drinks with some coworkers. Then I went back to the hotel to grab some dessert and settle in. The hotel had this incredible berries and cream dish and I had bellied up to the lobby bar to have that and a nightcap before putting myself to bed after a long week of meetings and presentations. I remembered exchanging business cards with some other business travelers at the bar. A bald guy a few stools down on my left and a small woman next to me on the right. We had commiserated about work travel and winter and how this hotel had a nice lobby. It all started so wholesome, but somewhere along the way, my plans for a delightful slightly tipsy evening were usurped by a bacchanal, and my knees, wallet, and blue jeans were sacrificed at the altar.

"Listen, I'm just glad you're okay. You said you would try to make a move after we talked, you said you were heading out and back to the hotel."

Back to the hotel?

Okay, so I left my berries and cream dessert and wandered blindly into the streets with strangers. Her call sent me out into the icy winter night, wandering incoherently back to the hotel. The opportune ankle twist must have brought my mind back online long enough to make a beeline for the lobby. Thank God for friends, cell phones, and adrenaline.

I brushed my teeth and packed my muddy clothes into my suitcase with my nice, unsoiled work garb. Checking out of the hotel, the front desk clerk asked how my stay was. My pleasantry reserves were low. I answered honestly. I told them I had kind of a weird night, that something messed up might have happened.

"Oh! Yeah! We heard about you," the desk clerk quipped.

I raised a heavy eyebrow, inviting them to expand.

"You came into the lobby, and these people walked in behind you. They told the security guard they could take you to your room."

"Was it a bald guy and a tiny Asian woman?" I asked, remembering the people I met while indulging in my dessert before everything went down. "Yeah, yeah, sounds right. It was a woman and two men."

Two men.

A blurry memory snapped to the front of my brain. *The security guard!* Through the fog I remembered crying in my room, emptying my wallet and shoving wadded cash into his reluctant hands. No, he had said, this is my job. But I had insisted. He had saved me with a supervised elevator ride, away from people I did not know who wanted to take me to my room.

The picture emerged. Yes, I had been drinking, but I sat down at the bar for dessert, I was lucid. I was chatting with people who I thought were also there, on their own. That's when the night ended. The night went black until the soggy chill of a mud puddle seeping into my back as I stared up at the low gray winter night sky, hobbled by a tipsy ankle strapped to a high heel. I was running away from something. The ankle twist woke me up long enough to get me back to the hotel and into the domain of a security guard. I had begged him to get me to my room.

He was annoyed with me. I was crying. I couldn't thank him enough and shoved all the money I had into his hands, because he had saved me.

The unremembered parts were murky. There were predators lurking in the darkness of what I couldn't recall. Tears began to well up hotly behind my cheeks as the realization clicked into place. The girl at the front desk looked at me wide-eyed and offered me a donut from their break room. I said no because my phone was buzzing, because my cab was outside to take me to the airport. I reeled in the backseat, recapped what I knew out loud to the driver, who didn't care.

"God, I must have drank more than I thought. I really don't think so, though. Do you think…? No…no way. I'm sure nothing bad happened. It was just a bad night. But it's so weird. And not like me! I swear…" I stared out the window at the Minnesota billboards for rehab clinics and university pre-med programs. I couldn't shake the fear that I had lost something.

By the time I checked in for my flight, the gravity set in. My stomach sank like I missed a step on a staircase. I shook with retroactive terror. I was more than used to hobbling around weird cities in various states of intoxication, but nothing bad ever happened. Nothing that a little greasy breakfast and some mea culpa phone calls couldn't fix. This time was different. It felt like I had brushed with something sinister.

I called my mom and told her what I knew.

"Oh no, sweetheart. What are you going to do?"

"I'm going to get the hell out of Minneapolis."

"No. Whitney. I mean. Are you going to call the police?"

I thought about the implications of her question. On one hand, if what I believe happened was true, that two people conned me at a hotel bar and attempted to get me back to my room to rob me or worse, then going to the police was a noble (if ineffective) path. But a voice in the back of my mind replayed the warped and damaged tapes of prior nights out, planting a very real seed that maybe I hadn't gotten roofied by some savvy midwest con artists but really just got hammered and resisted the kindness of strangers who tried to help me get back to safety after I collapsed in the street.

"Honey, I hate to even ask this, but..."

"What? Mom."

"Do you feel...molested?"

I shuddered and felt the brush of a near-miss again. I did not feel molested. Hotel footage would validate that I'd been escorted bravely by a monstrous security guard to my room, alone.

The fear intensified and I began doubting my own story. My gut feeling, Patti's reaction, the anomalous memory loss and unfamiliar queasiness told a story of a brush with real danger. Even with the muddy mountain of evidence stacked on that hotel room desk chair, it could have been just another morning as a confused and self-destructive twenty-something. I thanked my embattled guardian angel for getting me through another round of shenanigans as I doubted myself. Drenched in shame, I knew that it was just as likely that I was not a victim, just a mess. Neither of the viable truths was comfortable.

I coped the only way I knew how. At 11am on a wintry Wednesday, I walked across the freshly buffed airport floor and took a seat at the bar.

Rock Bottom

Rock bottom was imminent. I kept waiting for the moment where I knew, beyond the shadow of a doubt, that I needed to make a serious change, but it never came. I never hit the kind of rock bottom you hear about in meetings or shows about addiction. I had no messy divorce, no homelessness, no time spent 'down and out.'

For years, I had held onto those lacks as evidence that I didn't have a problem. It let me kick the can down the road and do what I knew would be hard work at some nebulous future date. In the meantime, I tried to convince myself that a stern judge evaluating my life with a clipboard would run through her checklist of all the common tropes of problem drinkers and she would come up empty. The only real evidence of drinking too much, I posited, was how I consistently drank too much. I did routinely throw any chance of tomorrow to the dogs so I could have a more interesting right now. But that was it, really.

I convinced myself I drank because I was bored, and continued to pile on distractions to keep myself in a low-level of chaos that ensured I would never have the time or clarity to hear the guidance of the nagging voice inside. I chose societally acceptable means of distraction like working too much and traveling. Devoting myself to those, I could convince myself that I was satisfying my hunger for meaning and connection. They delivered a watered-down, single-serving dose of each that I thought kept me satiated. I ached for something bigger, something more out of life, I wanted the kind of deep connection with others where you could share your deepest, darkest secrets. Drinking was my high-speed train to connection that didn't require any real vulnerability.

I let drinking lie to me about being an adult. Truly, it was just my chosen method of playing dress-up, where I could assume the identity I associated with whatever I was drinking. By shifting my method of inebriation, I stepped into a different life to see if it worked better. I gave them all an honest go. I clinked glasses of dry rosé with friends over fancy appetizers to play-act sophistication. I downed pint after pint of heavy hoppy IPA, convinced I enjoyed them while I played the role of believable guy's girl. The trappings of bar culture became a monstrous sucking sinkhole of time, energy, and potential.

For years my favorite hobby was watching NFL football. It was only ever tangentially about the football itself. Really, it was about feeling connected. It was drinking heavy beers and housing bacon cheeseburgers and bitching deftly about my injured running back. I was part of a family, united in black, gold, and shared hatred for the Baltimore Ravens. It was about that and bantering with the boys in the bar. It was about proving to them via continuous acts of coolness that I was worthy of their time.

When I donned the colors and screamed at some hapless referee through the TV, I felt like I was part of something. I was tapping into my family history and a national legacy. Spectator sports also fast-tracked friendship by skipping the nuances of human connection entirely. I identified my allies and enemies by the colors of their jerseys and the closeness of their reactions to play calls as my own. It felt like a cheat code for making the kind of friends that you loved intensely for one afternoon and then never saw again.

This was a lifestyle that did not love me back. One late night after a Super Bowl party, the February wind cut across the prairie and brought the air temperature well below zero. I was warmed by bourbon and hubris and demonstrated my dedication to the up-for-anything persona by bringing some friends home and deciding to break into the hot tub in my apartment complex. We scaled the gate and jumped into the water, realizing too late that they didn't heat the hot tub in the winter. Panic set in and I leapt out of the cold water. A friend, watching bewildered from the sidelines, offered me my boots. But I was in an unhinged state of fight-or-flight and immediately jumped the fence again, too hopped up on adrenaline to properly dry or dress myself. I ran a quarter mile home barefoot on icy asphalt and woke up the next day to find the bottoms of my feet replaced by swollen, frostbitten blisters. I massaged them in coconut oil and warmed them by my gas fireplace and it sunk in that trying this hard to be cool felt terrible.

The beliefs I held about myself, about the need to be cool and capable, were my security blanket. Underneath them was a feeling that there was something painful and true that I couldn't quite reach. I tried tapping into it in therapy, by reading self-help books, adopting new agey hobbies like astrology, enneagrams, and other mechanisms of self-understanding. It seemed like I was doing everything right, on paper. According to sitcoms and beer commercials, I was doing the right things. But my feet were throbbing and my brain felt like a shopping cart with one misaligned wheel that made the whole thing list ceaselessly to the left.

I tried on more personas. I got my aura cleansed. I learned to meditate. I started weight training. I drank green smoothies. I tried to do anything that would fix that squeaky wheel. When I felt the urge to make a change, I adopted new habits and identities whole-bodily. I committed to things that would become the pillars of my life until it was time to burn them down and replace them unceremoniously with whatever came next. But all those new things did was make me feel more busy and somehow further from myself. I was still trying too hard, just in cuter ways, and it felt like it was doing the exact opposite of what I wanted it to. I wanted to feel at ease. I wanted to stop feeling like my head was caving in. I wanted to stop trying to figure out who I was by constructing a persona inspired by pop culture. The more I tried, the further I felt from the truth.

I craved tangible ways to feel more comfortable in my own skin, and I was willing to do anything I could, except, of course, listen to my own body, which told me over and over that it was time to quit drinking. I hoped that something outside of me would tell me what was wrong with me so that I could go ahead and fix it once and for all like a leaky shower. I hoped the solution was something simple like cutting carbs or getting up earlier. I did absolutely everything I could to stay in my head and out of touch with my own body.

I drank (and drank), ate, kissed, and cried my way through so many todays until I almost ran out. My dedication to lying to myself was a locked cage and the swallowed key passed slowly through my digestive tract, wreaking havoc. At some point, my body screamed that I needed to stop sacrificing tomorrow for a more interesting today.

I believed that to do something meant doing it all the way, so that mythical ideal of just drinking in "moderation" was a no-go. I preferred instead to swing wildly from all to nothing.

Villain

Years of subsequent self-awareness practices have revealed that my brain is a high-efficiency manufacturer of problems and a key producer of self-doubt. The sophistication with which I have engaged in self-sabotage leads me to believe I am not just a playful antagonist but likely a supervillain in my own life. While autonomous problem production is impressively powerful, the workload it produces is overwhelming to the market. I habitually question my own motives. I ritualistically and humbly backpedal in the face of irrational what-ifisms that I've conjured not from reality but from a fear-filled sludge pit of my own imagination.

If I were planning a life for someone I despised, I would force upon them many of the choices I have made for myself (a person I claim to like) with considerable assistance from my calculating villain brain. On a stormy Saturday morning, I decided to make four recipes at once. Four gluten-free, ketogenic desserts for a cookie exchange later that day. This activity combined several of my most antagonistic traits: procrastination, over-promising, and aggressively evangelizing my personal beliefs onto others, in this case using the medium of baked goods.

The plan: fudgy low-carb sea salt brownies, dark chocolate dipped maple bacon, key lime bars, and a gluten-free take on the classic chocolate chip cookie. Ultimately, I ended up with empty hands, a smoky kitchen, and a crushed spirit.

I had every intention of walking into this cookie exchange like a triumphant warrior queen returning from conquest, balancing several trays of impeccable *("and so good for you!")* desserts. I believed I would incite a revolution that left the stale paradigms of baking, dieting, and Saturday socializing in my wake. But when the first recipe, a "fudgy" ersatz brownie came out of the oven a dripping mess, my reality began to crumble like almond flour in room-temperature coconut oil.

The kitchen filled with smoke as I dumped the greasy sludge into the trash. The fake sugar in the dark chocolate-dipped bacon was igniting violently under the broiler, sending angry plumes of failure billowing from the oven. The charred remains of crispy-pork-that-never-was followed the brownie sludge into the trash.

The third mishap occurred because I failed to realize prior to this undertaking that gluten-free baking is a goddamned lie. These egregious bloggers who encouraged me to follow in their fraudulent footsteps should be held accountable for leading us astray. I chiseled the wheatless abominations from the pan to which they had, in burnt solidarity, swiftly, permanently adhered themselves.

The final dish, a coconut key lime bar, turned out pretty good actually. But they were aesthetically godawful, better suited to eating out of a pan over the sink with a spatula in the middle of the night, not displayed next to immaculate gingerbread men and women. The clock on the wall told me that the cookie exchange had started an hour ago. I had nothing to show for it.

I walked there through rain that was as icy as my mood, punishing myself for thinking I could ever smash the cookie patriarchy. Flour, sugar, and Big Cookie had won a battle they didn't even know they were fighting. I was David stabbing Goliath's toe with a brownie-encrusted toothpick.

Now, back to the fact of being a self-made problem-haver, an entrepreneur of sabotage. In my fury of kitchen productivity, I set out to chop a bar of Baker's chocolate into meltable chunks for the dipped bacon. With my chef's knife against the solid mass, I leaned on the dull edge with the heel of my hand to break it into pieces. At that moment, it occurred to me that the blunt edge of the knife may be better suited to the task, so I flipped the knife over so the sharp side faced up. Without thinking, I lifted my other hand, rose onto the balls of my feet in preparation of bringing my body weight down to support the downward pressure on the chocolate, and was about to set my hand, with my full weight, down on the business end of a chef's knife.

Somewhere in the far reaches of heaven, my guardian angel woke with a start from a buzzed beach nap and knocked wildly on the inside of my skull. The moment of realization felt like when your socked feet slide down the edge of one carpeted step to the next. Everything was fine, but I wanted to scream.

My villain brain saved that image of my hand coming deliberately down onto the sharp blade of my upturned knife and she played it for me in HD several times a day. She seemed to derive great joy from bringing up painful moments like those for me to relive and squirm in my own self-hatred. She compiled scrapbooks full of flubbed words, angry stares from strangers in traffic and statements that didn't hit their intended recipient quite right. She rejoiced in replaying the tape to torture me with the hope of changing the outcome, or being better prepared for a next time that doesn't exist. Ultimately, she wanted me stuck in the cringey past or tripping on the fearful future. She hated to see me in the flow so much that she'd pull me out of it with jarring thoughts like *What if you woke up tomorrow and you were blind?*

She wanted me freaked out, my head on a swivel, because she doesn't believe I have what it takes to protect her. She doesn't trust me to feel my way through the day. She had good reason. I used to drown her voice in liquor. I made a hobby of delegitimizing her. I tried everything to shut her up and keep us separate. When I discovered that she was just about the business of self-preservation, I started proving her wrong. After all, my fingers didn't get sliced off that day. I also didn't get shunned for not showing up with three trays of cookies. Everything was fine. We saw, together, that the world can be kind.

Villain brain is often wrong-thinking, but I chose not to banish her, because she's got some great attributes. She's incredibly detailed. The horror-scapes she paints for me are Lynchian in their complexity. She's a talented strategist with blueprints and schematics of every possible thing that can go wrong for me. She's tireless in her constant, tactful navigation of minefields that have never actually existed. She is a good resource, in a toxic environment. If I re-assigned her, perhaps we could both thrive.

Snakes

I was mentally and physically exhausted from running on the fear treadmill and keeping my guard up against everything and everyone all the time. I went back to therapy. Making the appointment was half the battle. I girded my loins and prepared for a therapist to read between the lines of my stories and tell me something I didn't know, to unearth some hidden hard truths that I'd gone blind to.

I was prepared to adapt to painful realities. After all, I did it every time we moved, every few years, my whole life. I was so used to being uprooted and shocked that I came to expect it. What I couldn't do, under any guidance or circumstances, was sit still. I was nearly incapable of doing nothing. I believed I could handle hard truths, but not uncertainty. Uncertainty was the feeling that I drank to ignore. Behind uncertainty was the feeling of being blindsided and feeling foolish. There was shame in uncertainty. Years of public schooling and standardized tests had ingrained the belief that there was virtue—and safety—in knowing.

But the world did not always feel knowable. A mischievous voice in my head liked to chime in to remind me exactly how insane it is to just be alive. *Isn't it weird how we might all perceive color differently? Did you ever notice how time goes faster the older you get?*

When that happened, I couldn't take it. Tuning into the insane nature of reality felt like being dosed with psychedelics at an important board meeting.

I was supposed to be keeping it together, but the swirling and magical nature of reality really wanted me to party. The disconnect between my order-craving brain and the part that wanted to traverse the weird would clash and send me spiraling into full-body freakouts. It shook my core and left me feeling as disconnected and ungrounded as ever.

Making room for uncertainty felt like going over Niagara Falls in a glass barrel. If I didn't know what was coming, all I knew was that it was likely to be excruciating. *What if my car flew off the road? What if I choked on a nacho and died alone in dirty sweatpants? What if I was going insane?*

This—my third—therapist's office was a musty attic with embroidered pillows scattered across dirty wall-to-wall carpeting. She had me sit in a chair that was like a beanbag, where I shifted awkwardly and watched dust float in a sunbeam while she explained that the things I was afraid of were *irrational*. Each time I had a fearful ideation that began with the phrase "what if," she declared I was "indulging in irrational thoughts."

Her certainty in the matter was exactly like that beanbag chair, soothing at first, but increasingly uncomfortable the longer I sat in it. I misapplied her advice and chastised my next panic attack. "You don't make sense!" I cried, like the desperate next victim in a horror movie, but it didn't stop. Even as I berated my anxiety for being illogical, it kept right on fraying my nerves. Not only did the fear *not* go away when I understood that it was baseless, now I also felt bad for being afraid in the first place. I wasn't just scared anymore, now I was stupid, too.

I tried to plead my case to the therapist but attempting to speak with conviction and poise was impossible from my prone position in the beanbag. I wasn't irrational! If anything, *she* was the irrational one, didn't she watch the news? If she was doing her civic duty by keeping up with current events, she would know that freaky stuff happens *constantly*.

When the Aurora movie theater shooting happened twenty miles from my house, the massacre and subsequent trial occupied the news cycle for months.

We speculated, tried to explain the how and the why, until something new happened and that spectacularly violent, upsetting story gave way to the next one. Staying informed apparently meant intentionally overdosing on a never-ending supply of other people's trauma.

Before dawn a few months later, I was driving to catch a flight from Denver International when the BBC World Service felt the need to tell me that a man was caught trying to cross the border into Afghanistan with a duffel bag full of human heads, then handed the mic over to my local station for traffic and weather. I wondered why they were allowed to just casually dump that horrifying image in my lap and leave me to continue my commute. At the airport, the news showed footage of more violence in the Middle East. It was 7am. I drank coffee and a bourbon. The bartender made a joke about my "Elvis breakfast" and I pictured myself dying on a toilet.

By the way, bathrooms are supposed to be a refuge, which makes stories about something going wrong in that vulnerable moment especially enticing to the news media, like when a python makes a wrong turn in the sewer and ends up in a toilet bowl. Pay attention to the news long enough and you'll see a version of this story trotted (or should I say slithered) out again and again. Some poor fool comes home from work and opens the lid to find the bowl wholly occupied by an impossible reptilian invasion. The anchors smirk and share the wild and wacky story, "Local plumber discovers an entirely *different* kind of snake in this quiet suburban home. Find out what this means for your family, after the break."

The snake-in-the-toilet trope is one of the fearmongers' greatest hits. It forces you to reconcile the staggering number of perfectly-timed impossibilities that had to happen. It takes a relatable situation and offers a visceral reason to fear it. It erodes faith in the sanitation department.

After hearing this report of a reptile's fatefully wrong turn, you approach the toilet with ready trepidation like Indiana Jones, and open the lid with your toe, just in case.

Outlandish news delivered daily by dead-eyed anchors suggests the unfathomable ubiquity of mayhem.

In a clickbait-driven world, it's easy to believe that crazy stuff happens all the time. So when I got home from the dusty beanbag hellhole that day, I was mad. I wanted to know how exactly my fears were irrational when life felt like a swirling abyss of insanity. *What was an irrational fear in an increasingly irrational world?* If people can get massacred at the movies and a python can emerge from the plumbing, then I am well within my rights to have my hackles up 24/7.

Under conditions of normalized stress and overstimulation, it doesn't take much for "irrational" fears to seem very real. For me, sensational stories stacked on top of Stranger Danger and Campus Rape Culture, and I learned to live as if there *was* a python in the porcelain.

When I am in the thick of a panicky day, I will beg, pray, plead for my anxiety to just go away. But fear can't go away, because I still need it. The fear response helped my ancestors fight or flee from saber-tooth tigers, while my fears were born from a thousand "be carefuls" shouted after me in childhood, traumatic news footage, and the rumination of a restless brain. Somewhere along the way, my sensitivity knob got turned up to eleven and everything became a tiger or a trick or a toilet python.

Indulgence in worst-case scenarios was my misguided attempt to stay safe. I believed that if I could imagine the worst, I could prepare for it. In the process, I scared myself over and over and created mayhem in my mind that I tried to shove to the back corner and ignore. Emboldened by darkness and neglect, fear took on an unreal magnitude and cast a shadow over my whole life. After being shaken daily by panic attacks for years, and working with my fourth and fifth therapists, I understood that my anxieties were not some outside invader to trap and torture, but a part of my mind that I tried to reject. By rejecting my fear, I was rejecting myself. Of course I was stuck.

Something shifted when I took responsibility for creating the toilet python, and recognized that I could also render it an easily flushable earthworm. I just needed to be brave enough to open the lid and look. Approaching my fear with curiosity made it shrink in magnitude and intensity. I learned to leverage invasive thoughts out of my subconscious.

Patti is petrified of raccoons because a feisty little trash panda once leapt out of a trash can at her. This was one instant, a drop in an ocean, of a whole life of experiences that were otherwise raccoon-free. But the fear became entrenched and when I knew her she would quiver at the mere mention of the r-word. Her toilet python, her vicious prank, was a raccoon in every trash can. In her mind, every trash panda that scampered from our headlights slavered rabidly with visions of sinking their razor-sharp teeth into her jugular. What if she got bitten? What if she caught rabies and turned into a brain-hungry zombie? What if, what if, what if? Only my distance helped me see the ridiculousness of her fear, but it wasn't ridiculous to her. She felt it in her bones.

When the brain falls into the habit of fear, it needs gentle leverage—not rationality—to change it. I couldn't reason my friend out of her trash bandit phobia, just like I couldn't *think* my way out of the fear of being pranked, or murdered, or sex-trafficked. I couldn't surgically extract a rotten what-if from my mind, I needed to nudge it ever so slightly until it broke free. So, the next time my brain presented me with a what-if, I wiggled it with a reframe.

What if the supervolcano under Yellowstone erupts and plunges us into volcanic winter? What if we run out of food and have to resort to cannibalism?

"OR..." I offered in response, "What if I log into my bank account and there's a million dollars there?" I let my imagination work for me instead of against me. If I was going to be delusional anyway, the least I could do was indulge in some fun, life-affirming delusions. I felt powerful! And I leaned into crafting alternate scenarios to counter the frightening what-ifs.

What if my dog revealed that he was the crown prince of Estonia, living under a witch's curse?

What if I invited Drake to my birthday party and he showed up with a Bengal tiger on a leash?

What if it started raining glitter?

Reframes were fun, and eventually the nagging what-iffery began to subside. I noticed. I accepted. I shifted. I regained control of my inner narrative and re-discovered that my mind was still powerful despite having some bad habits. We started playing for the same team again and eventually, I welcomed the what-ifs because they presented an opportunity to respond heartily with a new, more fun YEAH, WHAT IF of my own.

I accepted that the end goal of healing is not to never feel anxious again, but rather to build a solid enough foundation that fear can come and go without ruining my day. Fear made me walk boldly toward what scared me and trust my ability to handle whatever happened. It is taking time, tons of patience, and allowing lots of little steps toward and through fear. But what happens if I continue to choose faith over fear? What if the answer is freedom?

Cooperation

There is no winning against villain brains. There is only acceptance. I've re-assigned her. We are optimizing resources. To cooperate with her, I am simply requesting a moratorium on her production of problems including but not limited to psychosomatic symptoms of illness, financial woes, and the emotional turmoil of others.

Instead, we will focus together on producing solely one product from this moment on, and that is a profound and actionable trust. We will soon find out if a frightened, suspicious, cynical villain can use her powers to dream up blessings.

Resolve

When I knew my enemy—that villain brain—it was easier to mount a campaign against it. I could begin to understand its motivations. That knowing made me feel ever-so-slightly more in control, although the lingering well of fear and doubt deep within me still begged to be addressed. I knew it was time to bring it to light because I was finally exhausted. Crying with strangers and throwing up at airports had lost all of its charm. The cycle of shame had officially gotten old. I was continually fifteen to thirty pounds overweight, bleary-eyed, and tired. I was bored with apologizing for myself when my toughness—a product of deep insecurity and directionlessness—came out as rudeness. Confused with where I stood, I acted like a huge bitch. Kind of a lot. It wasn't authentic, but it was very, very real.

I was always tentative and embarrassed when I called my friends to preemptively apologize for burning bridges with dumb banter or sloppy behavior. Under the influence I experienced waves of anger fueled by a feeling of being less-than. I saw happy people and hated them, and the anger spewed forth in caustic comments and daggery gazes that barely registered on anyone else's radar, but made me feel cool and powerful. In reality, I was just some sloppy chick talking shit about a football team. I had no power. I was floundering.

It took a gargantuan level of effort to justify my own behavior to myself. I jumped through mental hoops about being too smart to fit in, or just naturally being a loner. It wasn't true, and I knew it, and the effort to maintain the lie depleted my batteries and contributed to the sluggishness that was already pre-cipitated by my diet of Manhattans and the sandwiches I ate in bed to nurse my hangovers.

I was burnt out on the constant low to mid level hum of chaos that made my everyday feel like a slog. Even when I was just going through the motions, I was doing it on hard mode. I was living with the handbrake on. I didn't like myself. I was lonely, confused, and I didn't see a way out.

I wanted to change, and the biggest impediments to change were my own delusions. I had to get out of my own way. For years, I resisted quitting because of my preconceived notions about what sobriety looked like. I pictured lots of crying and firm-jawed proclamations in brightly-lit church basements. It never occurred to me that I could do sobriety in whatever way I wanted, that it could include staying up late, meeting people, being creative, and finally tapping into all that potential the teabags and horoscopes told me I had.

I believed I needed an entirely new identity, because the one I had was broken. It was self-defeating. I thought I wanted adventure and greatness, but my actions led me to blurry boredom. I was curious about the disconnect, and so enlisted the help of a professional. I went back to therapy.

My fourth therapist was small and mean and I loved her because I knew she wasn't lying to me. She raised botoxed eyebrows at the excuses that even I didn't believe anymore. I told her how I didn't want to wake up on my thirtieth birthday feeling woozy and ashamed of whatever celebratory shenanigans I had gotten into. I was sick of my own bullshit, my own desperation and inabil-ity to deliver on my desires to lose weight, save money, have better clothes, and live a better life. I was tired of not being able to make things happen. I was over being the kind of person that things happened to. She handed me her ear-marked copy of *Above the Influence*—a vintage health resource that showed its age with references to margarine as a healthy alternative to butter. When I got to the chapter about the physical toll of mid and late stage alcoholism, a switch flipped. The graphic description of sagging, sallow skin and a torso filled with goo as a condition called ascites kicked in was all it took. In that moment, my shallowness was a saving grace. The fear of being ugly pushed me over the edge and I made the choice that I had avoided for years. It was Leap Day, February 29th. I was 29 years old.

When I finally quit, it was partially because I could no longer ignore the inner voice that started calling me on my lies, snorting indignantly each time I justified reaching for the bottle because I was bored or had a "naturally high tolerance." I already wasn't fooling anyone, and finally, I wasn't fooling myself. The time came to accept that I was in full control of my life, which meant taking drastic measures to live according to that deep, all-or-nothing integrity that bubbled beneath the surface, hungering for something real.

Ice Cream

For the first thirty days of sobriety, I ate a pint of Ben & Jerry's ice cream every single day. I remember the ritual viscerally. They had come out with the "Core" line that had a habit-forming cookie dough or fudge center. Walking to the grocery store for my nightly pint replaced the ritual of walking to the liquor store for a six-pack or whatever and the sugar high replaced the lost carbs from the alcohol. Previously, I might have berated myself for these dietary indiscretions, but I was letting my body figure itself out. I tried to trust its instincts. I let the ice cream flow and the need for that insane amount of sugar resided naturally. Then I tapered down to a handful of Trader Joe's peanut butter cups, then eventually to a square of dark chocolate, and then to nothing.

I barely knew what to do with myself in that first year of evenings, but I was giddy with the possibilities. One night, I ran out of toothpaste, and the realization that I could get in my car and safely drive to Target at 9pm was a revelation. Talk about *freedom*. I could literally do anything.

I sat down to watch TV and was instantly bored. I understood why I needed to be impaired to consume hours upon hours of mindless mass-produced entertainment. It was empty calories for my brain, and I used to consume them endlessly. Now that I was letting my brain stay online in the evenings, it required some more potent, nutrient-dense stimulation. I bought adult coloring books and logged in to online forums for people in the process of quitting drinking. I took my dog for longer walks.

I went to bed earlier to spend more time with the fascinating life I lived on the other side. I reveled in the full nights of sleep, uninterrupted by the thrashing and sweating of the drinker's dawn. Mornings were a revelation. To wake up clear headed, unashamed—in full possession of my dignity, wallet, and phone—I felt like a goddamn superhero.

I hit thirty days sober and my tiny therapist winked and said, "I betcha can't make it to sixty!" It was on. By sixty days I felt superhuman. I was sleeping better and had more mental clarity. I had energy and wasn't locked into a perpetual blood sugar rollercoaster. The good feelings were their own reward, but I had the urge to reward myself for my accomplishments with something that wasn't bottled and bubbly.

At three months, I bought myself a membership to the Wild Animal Sanctuary, a park by the airport that provided a forever home to wild animals that had been kept in captivity. They homed hundreds of lions, grizzly bears, camels, tigers, and wolves in a facility that was respectful, non-exploitative, and beautiful. Almost every Sunday, I woke up early and drove out there to walk along the raised walkway and stare at the wild animals.

At six months, I got a tattoo. It has a design of the moon because I was reading about Carl Jung and the idea of circumambulation, the long roads we take and multiple perspectives we integrate toward reaching our potential. That's what I felt I was doing—walking circles around my experience and examining it from every angle. Watching the problem shift and change as I examined it through various lenses the way the moon changes in visibility but never in form. It's not a particularly special tattoo, but I got it for the experience, and because it felt empowering to make a knowingly dumb decision with a clear mind. I moved into the city and started traveling more, knowing that I could handle the risks of being out there now that I was keeping my head on straight. I felt good, but I felt alone.

Freedom

Navigating a non-drinking life became just another obstacle course of noticing and reframing my beliefs. I didn't half-ass drinking, and I wasn't going to half-ass sobriety, either. I went full-on.

The first thing I discovered was that nobody gave a damn about me. It was a liberating realization. The fear of social shame was one of the reasons I prolonged my drinking career longer than I needed to. I didn't quit, because I didn't want to make it weird. I worried that friends, coworkers, even family would judge my choice. I was afraid of that hot seat, of having to explain myself and my reasoning to people who might not understand. I figured people would sneer and crack jokes or worse: get really solemn and look at me like a bird with a broken wing. I imagined my friends thinking of me the way I thought of people who quit the bar life: as a fallen soldier, a quitter, a buzzkill, and I understood my own hypocrisy. I had raged against those who quit drinking before me. On the surface, I called them boring. Beneath, I recognized that they were walking a righteous path that I was not ready to follow, and that made me feel scared, less-than, left behind. So, I avoided the awkward questions that I wasn't prepared to answer as a wobbly-legged teetotaler. (Not to be confused with a wobbly-legged drunk, which they had notably gotten used to.) I was shocked and delighted when literally no one cared when I quit. No one called me on it, no one asked questions.

No one cared! What a relief. That nobody batted an eye meant I had total freedom. If no one really cared, I could do what I wanted! They were all so deeply entangled in their own stuff that my big life changes barely registered on their radar. The current carried all me the way past relief to suspicion and then sadness. I was at first let off the hook when no one cared, only to realize that I really wanted someone to care! Why didn't anyone care?

Calling my mom and telling her I was a few months sober was like a coming out, and she was unmoved. I told her I wasn't drinking, she said she wondered why I had ordered club soda the last time we had dinner together. She moved on. I pressed her for a reaction. Wasn't she interested, maybe impressed? She asked, "What am I supposed to do with this information?"

Maybe for the first time, I thought what I was doing mattered. Empowering myself to quit drinking was a big moment for me. It was an accomplishment and a big step. I wanted people to be interested in my big life steps. Moving around my whole life meant I was always the new kid, and I rarely stuck around long enough to give people the chance to care about me. Now, as an adult, I realized it was one of the things I wanted most. I decided to cultivate more people who would notice. The realization revealed the shallow and tenuous nature of many of my relationships—many of which were formed or nurtured at the bar. I had soothed my need for social interaction by collecting single-serving friends in bars, airports, and hotel lobbies. We shared powerful micro moments and then forgot about one another almost instantly. For years I hid in a self-made social cave, only emerging sporadically because I didn't want people to get too close. Deep down, because I wasn't proud of myself, I knew that letting people in meant exposing the truth of the pain I was in. Now, I was ready to let people care about me.

I craved depth; the intimacy of shared experiences with people who truly knew me. That meant letting people see all of me, but I wasn't even sure if I had seen all of me. I had a few ride-or-dies, but the realization that I needed to start fresh and re-enter the social scene as a whole new person (or return to being the kind of person that let myself be known) was overwhelming. I needed stronger connections to make it through the trials of an entirely new lifestyle. I quickly realized that I wasn't going to get unconditional support or recognition from the guy at the end of the bar or the girl crying in the bathroom stall. I needed to learn to let myself care about people, and let people care about me.

Meetings

My tiny therapist suggested twelve-step meetings and I gave them a shot. I get why a lot of people stick with the program. There is structure, there are certain expectations and a routine that you can rely on. The coffee's bad and the lighting sucks, but you know what to expect. My experience taught me that the comfort of routine is as temporary as a clean kitchen. It's a good thing, but it doesn't get you all the way there. I went into my first meeting wide open. I walked out shaken.

I loved being in a room with people who *got it*, but it felt like I needed to prove myself by memorizing mantras and strictly complying with their agreed-upon process. This flew in the face of my newly-chosen autonomy. I had made the choice to quit and to show up at the meetings. I also wanted to make the choices to navigate my own recovery.

I kept trying, thinking something would click. But after a handful of meetings in different neighborhoods, with different themed groups, I still couldn't get comfortable saying "My name is Whitney, and I am an alcoholic." You might read that and a big red sign in your mind flashes DENIAL DENIAL DENIAL. That's cool, you could be right. Still, I never got used to uttering words that felt like lies to gain acceptance in a room of strangers. I coughed out the words and launched quickly into whatever else I wanted to share. That *a-word* never resonated. It clamored through my mouth into the stale air. I felt like a fraud, with so many eyes on me. It's not that the definition didn't fit.

After all, if it stumbles like a drunk, if it tumbles like a drunk...but "alcoholic" just felt so *loaded*.

When I was drinking I would say with false confidence that I wasn't an alcoholic because I did not *do* the things I associated with alcoholism ('drinking alcohol' hilariously notwithstanding). I was not an alcoholic, I assured myself, because my apartment was clean, I had a good job. I wasn't an alcoholic, I was in my twenties! I wasn't an alcoholic like those winos at the bus station. Now, *that's* an alcoholic. No, not me, I sometimes got up early on the weekend to go hiking. Not remotely the behavior of an *a-word*.

I could plainly hear the hollowness of my argument, but still, when the time came and I finished the phrase 'Hi, my name is Whitney and..." I just couldn't do it. Not only did it not feel true, but I also had no way to quantifiably prove if the definition fit. There is no standard definition. People say *alcoholic* refers to a person who has a disease, but I've never been able to parse whether they got the disease from drinking too much or the disease lay dormant within them until they lifted a whiskey snifter to their lips enough times to activate it.

Did I have a disease that caused me to drink too much? Or did drinking too much give me a disease? My newly-clear mind reeled as I grasped for clean certainty in a label. I knew that if I could admit that I was an alcoholic, then doors would open in those meeting rooms. If I refused to accept it, I was pitting myself against the recovery establishment. By choosing to shirk the labels and skip the submission, I chose to go it alone, again.

After my third AA meeting, an elder cornered me in the parking lot to snarl contemptuously that my joyful share was counterproductive. I had no hope of recovery, she said, until I sank to her approved depths of sorrow and self-flagellation.

She chose to go by the book and had multiple years of sobriety under her belt. She was accomplished and worthy of celebration. She was also still living enmeshed in anger and shame. She was not one of the people I wanted to meet. After her reprisal I sidestepped Big Recovery to see what else was out there. Unlike the elder in her coffee breath cloud of misery, I would not live by the dictates of my wounds. I chose instead to sit with them, and let the pain transform into truth and hopefully, ultimately, happiness.

Dreams

After a year sober, I lost the drive to drink or prove myself, numb out, and hide behind a woozy veil of hops and bourbon. But I couldn't help but feel like the alcohol had not fully left my system. Even though drinking didn't leave me down and out, it left me haunted. The ghost rattled her chains to distract me from how far I had come. I learned to live with her.

Every now and again, I will go to sleep and dream that I am drinking again. When I wake up, usually feeling a little guilty and panicked by my imagined transgression, I will feel relief that it was just a dream, and I will soothe myself by opening the app on my phone that shows me how many days it has been since I quit drinking. Almost every time those drinking dreams happen, I am on or near some significant anniversary, like a 6-month mark or a day that ends in two or three zeroes.

I heard someone say in a meeting once that the dreams are just what happen when your brain decides to "clean out the attic." They are your sub-conscious flipping through old scrapbooks, stepping into the nostalgia of a bygone life, and asking if you want to keep those relics, or let them go.

It's like looking at old pictures. Only the good times got documented for posterity, and that was what appeared when your brain did the audit to bring them back up to be processed. Drinking dreams showed the romance of a glass of champagne at a wedding. They skipped the hot cigarette breath of the groomsman copping a feel on the dance floor.

The same went for how I thought about drinking. My perspective changed after quitting. I could see the bait-and-switch techniques more clearly. There was always a touch of romance at the beginning, an intention of artistry like a fine red paired with a succulent steak. But on the other side of the intention, when the artistry failed to reveal true inspiration, it was a story of searching, chasing, and taking it too far until there was a rottenness of desperate overdoing like teeth stained purple and breath turned rancid by too much cabernet.

I had spent the better part of a decade trying mostly in vain to extend the romance, dancing on the edge of overindulgence for as long as I could before falling off. And I did fall off. Often literally. When I stacked that loose ankle on top of high heels and danced in the swaying embrace of too many spirits, it usually rolled and dropped me in the middle of wherever I was. I shrugged off the shame of a bad night like a major league pitcher shakes off a botched close, taking the L and moving on. By 5pm, when the soreness dissipated from my ankle and I had put in another respectable workday, amnesia set in. I dusted myself off and got back on the mound, standing in the buzzing lights of the liquor store, weighing my options.

Herein lies the rub of all rubs.

I drank to avoid my feelings. So, when I chose to deliberately sit with the feelings I had chosen for years to stifle, numb, and avoid, what I encountered was not some sweet and easy journey of self-acceptance. The path was paved with broken glass that shredded my feet and left bloody footprints all over my life. When I stopped drowning my thoughts and feelings in a bloody mary oblivion, I had to look myself square in the face and figure out who the hell I was. When you stop deluding yourself, it's like waking a sleepwalker. They will try to punch you in the face. I sat in the hot soup of my own psyche with the escape hatch welded shut and began to recognize the extent of the lies I told and the masks I wore. I began to see the cumulation of mental energy I wasted just trying to keep up with myself. It was panic inducing.

Even after a year sober, I was as anxious as ever. I wasn't being rocked by night sweats and shame-overs, and I wasn't wracked by fear and guilt because I'd let strangers into my house, lost my keys, or shattered the screen on my phone, but I still couldn't get through a day without feeling that pulse-quickening fear that sent me running for home. Sobriety wasn't the end-all-be-all anxiety-knocker-outer I needed it to be.

I had stopped the bleeding, but I still needed to address the wounds. I set out to dismantle the patterns of behavior that had me hiding and lying to myself. The damage was in the years I spent living out of alignment with myself, afraid to look within, unsure of how to prioritize my voice.

I used to use alcohol to turn down the volume on my loud thoughts. Without the booze buffer, everything got a little louder. Freshly aware of everything around me, my natural anxiety hit a new high. I had forced myself to get comfortable with uncomfortable situations by drinking my way through them. I drank through the insecurity of college parties, the loneliness of solo travel, the awkwardness of friends who only sort of get you. I used booze as the lubricant to twist and contort myself into an image of who I thought I needed to be, and what I found was an unhappy person who wondered why she felt misunderstood as she routinely failed to understand herself. I needed to address and deconstruct those patterns of thinking, which meant sitting with them, confronting the tough emotions I didn't know how to feel. It meant learning to unravel and actually listen to the inner voice that had been quietly asking me for years to tune in by ringing in my ears and churning in my stomach.

I cry a lot more now. The old me didn't know how. She was locked up like a mollusk. Sometimes, the right blend of vodka and vermouth would bring it out of her, but she wouldn't learn much except to avoid vodka and vermouth. She never let me go deeper, so I had to meet her more than halfway on the battleground of my heart. I had to push past her reservations and give her a big hug and start asking if she could let me go.

I had built so many associations through the lens of drinking. Booze was how I related to the world. I could barely go anywhere without something or someone being reminiscent of a drinking experience. Restaurants, airports, parks, and movie theaters were tainted with foggy memories of how I used to participate in life half in the bag. The ghost of drunk Whitney lingered in the dark corners of the things I still wanted to do. The memories hung from situations like Spanish moss, and my sober self had to wade through, cut it down, and set it on fire. I was like the new kid in town once again, except now I had to walk through life with a completely different set of beliefs.

I stopped wanting to go to restaurants. Drunk Whitney's ghost winked at me as she spun in her barstool, chatting up the bartender, a sip away from some foolish display. She haunted me most viciously in the airport. Inside the terminal, where I used to feel bubbly and safe, where I used to make friends and tell stories, now I felt trapped. My aware mind latched onto the memory of my airport exploits without the gauzy hangover filter. In those long, gray hallways that felt like machine tubes, standing in polite society to check-in or pass through security, I felt like I might explode. I was terrified of standing in long lines with nowhere to go, forced to keep my cool as waves of anxiety bubbled up my throat. I clenched my teeth through each trip, gripped by fear, feeling like I might throw up or pass out like I used to. Clear-headed, the prospect wasn't quite so cute as I pretended it was when I was under the influence of breakfast margaritas and delusion.

Most perniciously, I equated drinking with the happiness of new friends, relaxation after a tough day, and satisfaction of a successful work week. Now, even those emotions are haunted by the sloppy ghost that makes me question if I've let my guard down too far. When I feel too happy or too relaxed there is a voice that pipes up and reminds me to be careful. I used to only feel carefree in that moment right before I had one drink too many. My mind remembered that association and reminded me to pump the brakes if I felt too relaxed. The brain is a creature of habit. Even years later, it associates relaxation with inebriation. That guardian angel sits up straight and takes notice when she feels me letting my guard down. I'm still working on proving to her that I can be trusted now. I know that wasn't always the case.

Called Up

Two years into sobriety, everything was going totally great, except I still felt like garbage. It didn't make any sense. I had a good job. I was traveling and seeing cool places. I got to spend time with my family. I had friends all over the world. I believed myself to be an interesting person, or was at least trying my best to be. And yet.

I was still scared all the time. I would be going about my day as usual and suddenly get hit with a wave of panic that would bring me to a screeching halt. Panic attacks had been ever present in my life since that day at the hot dog stand in college, and probably before. I had thrown almost everything at them—I cut caffeine, I took deep breaths, I bought crystals and books and essential oils. I did yoga. I practiced gratitude. And still, the list of moments that could trigger a destabilization was vague and endless. Anything from the flicker of an overhead light to a sudden headache, glitch in the TV broadcast, random chest pressure, or a mean look from a stranger could send my mind into a spiral. My body quickly followed. My pulse raced, my skin crawled. I thought I might faint.

As soon as I rationalized myself to being okay with one thing, something else took its place. As I got more comfortable eating in public, waiting rooms became my kryptonite. When I got comfortable at the dentist, then driving on the highway became debilitating. I was particularly vulnerable to any experience that made me feel stuck. Airplanes, road construction, and formal events were waking nightmares.

I sought out therapist number five.

Then I met Maureen, who I hated for a while, because she was wholly unimpressed with the bonafides that I presented to her as I made my case for why my anxiety was bullshit and afflicting me for no reason. She was the first to be genuinely, infuriatingly disinterested in all of my proof.

"So why are you here?" she would ask, not letting me rationalize my way out of anxiety, and I had to confront that I was tired from chasing praise and my proof-gathering felt like an endless uphill Sisyphean push, and I understood that at the rate I was going I would never be enough, and I was sliding into despair. I got so frustrated to be confronted by that hard truth, that I was my own saboteur, that I just cried. And cried. (And cried.) When I went home I slept the rest of the day, feeling like that boulder had rolled back downhill and crushed me, because I'd let go and just felt my feelings.

Maureen knew how to make me cry, and scowl, and scream into a brightly colored pillow. She turned the key to some deep inner well of anxiety and unleashed wave upon wave of shaking, sobbing, shameful tears. When I'd straighten up and sniff and try to compose myself or apologize she would raise her eyebrows and let me know, like a mother pointing out the peas on her toddler's dinner plate, that I was not done. I sat in her warm biomat-covered chair and squirmed as she stared at me and asked me questions that I couldn't answer like, "Do you trust yourself?"

On her couch, I shed thirty years of stress tears that poured from a well that I dug by trying so goddamn hard all the goddamn time. She told me it was okay to just *be* and after three decades of doing, I didn't know what that meant. Doing was all I'd ever known, it was how I measured myself against other people, and how I knew if I was doing an okay job in life. If doing did not matter, I didn't know what a day was supposed to look like. She made me sit and feel. She made me remember how to breathe. For three months, I had to strap myself into a machine that showed my breathing pattern on a screen, which was great because I felt powerfully motivated to win that game, and so

I learned quickly how to breathe evenly. Soon, I stopped feeling like my head was going to pop off, I could connect with the rest of my body and recognize it as part of me.

After a year or so, I could almost hear her when she told me I could be anxious AND okay at the same time. She helped me discover that all the things that sent me into panic, the pains I would get in my stomach, the weird sensations up and down my spine, the tingling skin that WebMD was happy to suggest was some devastating autoimmune disease—these were called *feelings* and it was normal to have them. She told me that you could feel things—even bad things like anger and fear and loneliness and melancholy—and still be okay, still be a good person. She forced me to examine this idea that humans possess value irrespective of their actions and the number of achievements they collect. Even *mean* people, *unhealthy* people, *whiny* people, all the people that I viewed as a scourge, she believed had intrinsic value. I didn't buy it.

But every Tuesday morning, she opened my skull and waterboarded my brain with this idea until the seed began to sprout. I coughed and sputtered when I tried to repeat it. It made no sense. *My value is not determined by my accomplishments?* If I never accomplished anything again, if I gained weight and wore sweatpants to the grocery store and stopped writing and spent all the money I saved, I would still be worth something? How, exactly, would that work? How would I KNOW what I was worth and therefore how to carry myself through life?

She said I would still have value even if I couldn't pull a paycheck. Even if I got my legs chopped off and could not give my niece and nephew piggy back rides, I would still be a good aunt. She said, controversially, that it wasn't that important that I had a good sense of style or that I could make people laugh and tell a good travel story. I stared at her, beyond puzzled, "But it's cool that I AM those things, right?" She remained infuriatingly unimpressed by the bonafides that I wore as armor in every other part of my life. If all of these things that I used to objectively measure my importance in the world and the way I felt about myself mattered *less* than the fact that I was just a good person, *what the fuck was I even doing?*

That's why I downloaded apps where robots measured the symmetry of my face to tell me if I was pretty. I wanted them to give me the hard truth, so I'd *know*. I read self-help books so if ever I got into a relationship with someone I'd *know* if we'd get into murky interpersonal territory, and articles about the right net worth to reach in your thirties, so I'd know exactly how guilty to feel when I blew $300 on retinol creams and green tea bubble bath at Sephora.

Maureen, radical that she was, seemed to think I could wear footie pajamas and eat ice cream for breakfast and still be of value. It wouldn't matter if I wasn't always happy, that sometimes I felt sad or scared, I'd still be okay. While I looked at life as an obstacle course, a series of achievements to unlock and validations to collect, she would have me believe that I could *just be*, even if just being included getting rocked with a panic attack or eating too much caramel corn. She told me I could feel angry, sad, ashamed, or left out, and still be okay. My value was also not totally tied up with needing to be happy all the time.

With my worldview in question, I unraveled. I stopped clinging for dear life to this idea of proof-collecting. By no longer having to prove myself and who I was, I could start to let who I had always been shine through. It was rough. I had *no idea* what I liked, or what I wanted. I was back at my parents' house, choosing to travel full-time because traveling full-time sounded cool and made for an amazing, unclockable Instagram, *but was it what I wanted?* Did it make my inner child jump with glee, or was it another mechanism to impress and also distance my true self from any real, authentic connection, because I was afraid that letting people get close would just let them see the edges of the mask? Was I even wearing a mask anymore?

Slowly, those cool girl trappings began falling away. I had abandoned my aspirations of being the cool girl watching sports at the bar. My cool old truck stopped being worth the cost to repair. All my flannels were suddenly too big because when I quit drinking, weight just fell off my body without any effort whatsoever. Watching football sober was suddenly just a loop of brutality and corporate logos. I confronted the nagging suspicion that all of those things were mechanisms I had used to cope with the boredom of a mediocre life.

Perhaps, by raging against that so-called mediocrity, I held my feet to the fire to the point that I wouldn't ever have to worry about being mediocre, without knowing it. If I were mediocre by design, by my own chosen lack of will, then I could accept mediocrity as a byproduct. My greatest fear was to discover I had become mediocre by accident. That great fear and discomfort guided me to challenges, which gave way to growth, which provided some sense of comfort, for long enough to realize that comfort was the real mediocrity. My comfort zone was where I stopped expanding, stopped growing. Expanding beyond my comfort zone was the difference between the fake not-trying cool of movie characters and actual cool, which pushes past expectations and boundaries and makes the world their bitch in a cut-off Ride the Lightning t-shirt.

The thing about being *really* cool is not trying to be someone at all, and instead being wildly devoted to doing what you love according to the guidance of that true inner person that you don't have to try to be. This delicate balance of trying and not trying became the secret to my not-mediocre life.

When I quit drinking, I heard the mantra to "let go and let God." That was the hardest part. Trying and achieving always felt like action, and I knew that I could calibrate the degree of action. I was in the driver's seat and I was responsible for our destination. I felt strongly that I knew best and would use my brain to navigate, because I had worked hard to fill my brain with lots of information, and information was POWER. Therefore, if I was smart, I was also powerful. I could outsmart a transactional world that did not make sense to me, by working within its weird, foreign system. But recovery wanted me to let someone else drive? How would I *know* they were a good driver, and had my best interest in mind? Only I could know that! I was not in the business of "letting" anyone do anything!

Relaxing, trusting, flowing with the truth of who I was, listening to my body and my inner guidance, trusting my faculties and the universe, letting go and letting God all sounded more than far-fetched. It sounded outright dangerous. It felt safer to keep pushing. By doing the work that it took to objectively *know*—saving money, working hard, doing cardio, figuring out my diet, and identifying suitable leisure activities—I did actually strengthen some intrinsic confidence. So while measuring myself against others, or against myself in measurable ways, was not ideal from a healthy self-image perspective, the work it takes to win in those categories is the struggle that lays a foundation for my desirably not-mediocre life.

Ultimately, facing myself and the lies I believed was how I cracked open who I really am and what I really want. And what I want is…hell—I'll have to get back to you.

Luxe (Interlude)

To hell with golden harps, heaven is a stack of new cashmere, good denim, and buttery leather boots, punctuated by something dainty in rose gold and a mist of something that smells like earth. My Valhalla is comfortable aesthetic perfection, tags freshly removed.

Shopping. I like it. It taps perfectly into the primal drive to hunt and gather. The seeking, finding and consuming of the retail experience leaves me spent, satisfied. Depleted by bargain hunting and decision fatigue, my typically frantic mind is momentarily depleted. For a moment, it's quiet, though soon enough, the guilt will roll in. I will scold myself for robbing from my future, but for the moment I am calm, accomplished, and distracted by the novelty of the haul.

Picture it. It's Friday and I've been working hard. I woke up early. I did some kind of exercise and avoided the temptation to scroll through my phone. At work, I was nice to my coworkers and turned in high quality deliverables. I did my best, and now I need a release. But I quit drinking five years ago, so a trip to the department store steps up to fill the void left by happy hour. When the shopgirl greets me like a trusty bartender, we collaborate to do some damage not to my liver, but to my wallet.

There is cognitive dissonance as I recognize my self-destructive appetite for consumption. To cope, I pretend I'm not shopping for myself. I step into this fantasy that I'm the personal assistant of an incredibly wealthy woman who tasks me with finding her the best pieces for some upcoming event. This way, I'm not a glutton, simply the dutiful squire to a gorgeous megalomaniac, who just so happens to wear my same size. If I am cowed by an astronomical price tag I simply channel her and mutter our vague excuse—"Eh we already have something so similar to this," and place the decadent, suede pencil skirt back on the rack.

Perhaps, I muse, I am shopping for my future self, who happens to be casually, fabulously wealthy. But with each excursion and each jar of luxe frankincense-scented moisturizer, my present drains a little bit of life out of her. I am feasting on the blood of my future, in the name of looking chic at an upcoming event that is as imaginary as my successful lifestyle brand.

It's so good, that feeling of being surrounded by curated elegance, being invited to touch and try and experience and select that which connects with my essential nature. Some erudite, data-driven people in a distant branding department boardroom have predicted and broadcast my desires to me, and I am putty in their hands. My inner Veruca Salt touches everything and barely contains a tantrum. *"I want the world!"* I may be a bad egg, but outwardly I exhibit restraint, feign sophisticated, picky interest, but let the possibilities play in my head.

Perhaps, I consider, *this fresh lamb's wool sweater will transport me from my current life to that of the adventurous Canadian isle fisherwoman from the catalog.* Those marketing gurus channeled my rebellious spirit into soft muscle tees and high-waisted leather leggings. They answer my ache for elegance with soft gold hoops and winter layers. I buy their lie of consumerism and, often, I buy the sweater, too. It makes me feel temporarily powerful, like the wife of a recently murdered king.

It seems obvious that living out my galleria fantasy is in direct opposition to a destiny of *actual* wealth, sophistication, and power. In fact, indulging in short-term pleasures like thirty dollar candles creates a state of low-level crisis that contrasts starkly with the calm that flickering lavender flame was designed to impart. Post-shopping panic attacks are real, but at least they come wrapped in merino and silk.

So who cares if the indulgence in retail therapy flies in the face of long term goals? So what if I'm squandering the down payment for my hobby farm, a few roaming buffalo, a custom bungalow with wool insulation, a river stone hearth, and a giant writing desk with a view? Call it millennial disillusionment or abundance mindset, but since I can't *feel* that reality yet, I grasp for its trappings instead. Rather than stashing fifty dollars to grow the nest egg, I get the cargo pants I'll wear to paint the barn and a beef tallow candle that smells like cedar. When the real dream feels out of reach, I choose to play dress-up and dance with the ghost of the future.

Homeless

I was still looking for home everywhere except where I had a chance to find it. At the apex of the journey, to drive the point home, I became homeless on purpose.

I was living in Denver, and I had a nice apartment in this part of town that was a few tree-lined residential streets between a sprawling park and a main thoroughfare known for seediness.

On Sunday afternoons, the park pulsed with crowds gathered on picnic blankets for jazz concerts. Every other day it was abuzz with ultimate frisbee games and coming and going and running and dog-walking and stroller-pushing. I walked my dog around the lake and watched the sun dip behind the mountains and the lights flicker on in the high rises downtown and wondered how I could be in an objectively beautiful place, living an objectively enjoyable life, and still feel so unhappy.

To complete the circuit back to the apartment we weaved around to Colfax Ave which glowed under neon bar signs that cast the roving gangs of addicts in an ethereal glow. Crossing back into the neighborhood away from the speeding cars and methadone clinics was often a relief and, like my building, I felt held between two worlds. I didn't think I belonged to either. I had left the buzzing Colfax debauchery behind a year prior when I quit drinking and made a conscious effort to extricate myself from situations in which I might be ordering a patty melt and cheese fries at 3am. Meanwhile, the smiling faces at the park were all so picture perfect that I never believed them. I assumed there was some well of deep pain beneath their glossy exterior and I wanted to know it, but the Denver urbanite rarely cracked.

Work remained a constant. I had a full-time remote job for a cool tech company. I got to travel a decent amount, and collecting expanded responsibilities while also exploring new cities was exhilarating. I went to conferences in Vegas and Chicago, met up with coworkers in Austin and London, and networked with new friends who invited me to visit them in Mexico City. When I was drinking, I never would have said an impulsive yes to that kind of offer. I knew too well that an enticing invitation to a wild foreign city was a recipe for lost phones and mangled dignity. Sober, I was empowered. I could keep my wits about me. It was time to prove I could take the new skill global. It was a dream. Climbing the pyramids and walking the markets made me feel full in a completely new way. A summer thunderstorm clapped inches above our heads in the extreme, high-altitude climate and I practiced my rusty Spanish to procure churros. The city crackled with energy that I felt I could finally match after years of being dulled by the quiet weight of not just drinking, but the emotional heaviness that inspired me to drink in the first place. My curiosity for places and humanity roared back to life.

I floated back to Denver where a stack of mail including a credit card bill and my lease renewal notice brought me back to earth. The impromptu flight, the dog sitter, Airbnb, and adventure money had stacked up. Rent was increasing, although they assured me my rate was still very competitive, even undermarket, in the fast-growing city. I wasn't going to be able to pay rent and keep traveling.

The one-bedroom apartment that was both my home and my office was nice enough. I worked hard to make it cozy, spent money on furniture, cookware, and high-speed internet. Now I was kicking myself, knowing that money could have been spent on adventures. Suddenly, my place felt like a beautiful, beige prison.

Over Memorial Day weekend, I packed my things into a truck and drove to my parents place outside of Milwaukee. Their unfinished basement became a storage unit. They held a Welcome Home party for me during which I reminded everyone I was not "home."

I was just here to stash my stuff. It was a home base, nothing more. A life of clear-eyed adventure and heart-centered experience called.

The Volcano

For one of the first "big" trips, I was going to go to Bali. A few months before the trip, Mount Agung threatened to erupt. For weeks, the volcano gurgled and puffed smoke rings into the sky. Each morning, I tentatively checked the volcano's status. Half of me hoped she would blow before the trip so we'd be in the clear, the other half quietly prayed she would save the big show for us. Thousands of people lived on the side of the volcano and clung to her through the rumbles. News outlets chastised the inhabitants who refused to evacuate. They speculated death and destruction if orders went unheeded, but the Balinese remained steadfast. I admired how they clung to her through the rumbles. She didn't blow, and our trip went ahead as planned.

After thirty hours of transit through bustling LAX and mysteriously empty Shanghai, we landed in Bali. An air-conditioned van with *Goddess Retreats* inked in beautiful turquoise script on the side picked us up and shuttled us to a dreamy villa. For the next week, our every need would be catered to by an elegant staff of chefs, bodyworkers, and yoga teachers. Each day was anchored by sunrise yoga, with the rest of the hours scheduled to cultivate a perfect rhythm of exertion and relaxation. Expansive adventures like mountain biking, river rafting, and surfing were balanced by time dedicated to languishing by the sparkling pool or wandering the village. With my basic needs met, meals planned, and days scheduled, I had plenty of open headspace which I dedicated immediately to all of the things that could go wrong.

When I was invited to a yoga retreat in Bali, I imagined it was an extra brave way to run away from the stress and anxiety that was an everyday experience in my normal life. My job was tumultuous. Corporate leadership seemed to take pleasure in stirring the pot, restructuring teams and making roles obsolete. I knew my job was safe, but I also knew I would be the one to shoulder the burden as people fled the turmoil. I didn't want to shoulder more burdens, I wanted to travel. I wanted to work from anywhere and work enough to pay the bills so I had the time and means to explore.

I was splitting my time between my parents' house and various AirBnbs around the country in a sort of diet digital nomad lifestyle. Each morning at the family home, I woke up with a sense of dread and shame, considering that I was technically speaking, a thirty-year-old woman living with her parents. The arrangement worked, though, as a financial buffer for my traveling and to be supported while I cared for my dog, Koda.

Koda was a mutt with pure white fur and heterochromia. He had one blue eye and one brown, and I liked to joke that the blue eye could see into the future. He had been my ride-or-die through college, my first jobs, my first apartments. We had spent an amazing twelve years together. We went on thousands of great walks. He taught me commitment and responsibility. Through him, I learned that I was a capable and loving provider. When I went to Mexico City, he had stayed at an overnight boarding spot and came home with a bout of pneumonia that he couldn't seem to shake. For the last year, he had dealt with increasingly serious sinus infections. Each sneeze sounded foreboding. The stress and the vet bills piled up.

I was terrified of losing my roommate and confidant, but I also knew that on the other side of emotional devastation was a new type of freedom. I could save money. I could travel more. I could live purely for myself.

I hoped the trip to Bali would be a recalibration and an escape from nagging worry. I hoped it would relieve the stomach ache that I woke up with most days and plunged me into meta-worry about how the stress itself was ruining my health. I thought I could leave it behind, but the anxiety stowed away in my luggage. I didn't notice because my bags were overpacked with supplies I thought I needed to keep myself safe.

I usually lived according to the scout mantra: *always be prepared*. If I could imagine the worst case scenario, I figured, I could plan for it. So I packed for every trip, especially overseas travel, as if I expected my plane would crash and strand me on a desert island. I tucked snacks and waterproof matches between the silk and cashmere in my suitcase for a weekend at the Four Seasons. I tried to insulate myself against danger by planning ahead and packing supplies. I learned the word for "bathroom" in as many languages as I could. I tucked my passport into my bra. I went overboard, so if I actually did go overboard, I was ready with a warrior mindset and water purification tablets.

Planning was supposed to bring peace of mind, but it invited hypervigilance. When I was scanning my surroundings looking for danger, it was easy to think I had found it. The baggage was heavy. Buried inside my careful planning was a deep distrust of the people and places I claimed to want to get to know better.

While my travel companions sprawled on the beach and wondered out loud how they got so lucky to watch the sun set into the ocean behind rows of tanned and able-bodied surfers, I watched planes pass over and wondered how polluted the water was. We watched stray dogs frolic and nip at one another and I thought about mange. I adjusted my posture to hold my legs off the ground. I was in paradise, worrying about sand fleas.

At the twinkle-lit jungle villa, it was clear I would not need any of my prepacked prepper supplies. The food was exquisite, the company charming, and the bug spray plentiful. We got to know our retreat cohort around an elegantly decorated dinner table on a lanai and sampled fresh, colorful, delicious Balinese dishes. For a moment, as we laughed out loud and clinked coconuts, all was right with the world. We unpacked our suitcases into rattan bureaus in a bright and airy suite. The bathroom had a shower paved with riverstones with views of the jungle and a live gecko to eat the flies. It was elegant and natural in the exact way we wanted when we opted to come to Bali. We shut off the lights and tucked ourselves into our elegant mosquito-netted beds, repeating the mantras from post cards that were left for us on our pillowcases.

In the quiet darkness, my roommate's breathing slowed, and the worry that I had tamped down during dinner bubbled back up. I was overcome with exhaustion that reminded me how long it had taken to get here. We were literally on the opposite side of the planet. As far from home as I'd ever been. Though my cheeks burned from laughter at the dinner table, I considered the power of the tropical sun, which spiraled into ideation about fevers, parasites, and red hot volcano eruptions. Between freshly laundered white sheets, I let my mind run wild with vivid iterations of how the trip could still devolve into the kind of nightmare they make into a Travel Channel special.

I remembered the women cooking our fabulous meal in their outdoor kitchen and wondered how long the chicken sat out before being cooked. I remembered the children in the streets in the villages we passed on our way in, and the stagnant puddles we splashed through. My skin began to crawl. My stomach churned. Were we safe? Images of soiled hospitals, corrupt ambassadors, and Indonesian prisons danced in my mind, and I remembered the advice from the cheerful South African retreat host: *Be careful with your thoughts on Bali,* she said. *Things manifest quickly here.*

Her statement howled like a siren behind my intrusive thoughts. I was suddenly aware that my thought spiral was essentially a prayer for catastrophe. In Bali, my normal cohort of paranoid ruminations were stamped and delivered as priority mail, straight to the universe. I squeezed my eyes shut and tried to bleach my fears with pleasant images.

Sweet, deep magenta dragon fruit.

The embassies are closed.

Ginger tea with honey.

The doctor can't understand you and you're bleeding out.

The topaz tones of the Indian Ocean.

No one is coming to save you.

I crawled out of bed and fumbled in my kit bag for an orange bottle of little white pills to calm my mind and help me sleep. The doctors back home rolled their eyes and dismissed my questions about gut flora and ulcers, and sent me home with Ativan. I surrendered to their dismissive wisdom and popped a pill, nodding in recognition to the watchful gecko in the corner of the shower. The drugs stopped my racing thoughts and carried me to sleep.

On our third day in paradise, we were scheduled for a day trip. We were to cross a tide-dependent landbridge to a temple in the ocean. We were to dress in traditional Balinese garb to take in the site with style and reverence. They warned us ahead of time that anyone who was menstruating would not be able to attend. According to local myth, the last woman to set foot on Tanah Lot while on her moon caused the bridge to be destroyed in a violent storm.

The morning of the excursion, I woke to discover that my uterus was experiencing its own impeccably-timed high tide. I approached the retreat director to let her know I was sullied and no longer fit to worship at the ocean temple. While the other girls played dress-up in bright tapestries and white lace and posed for photos in front of the flowering hibiscus, I dipped my feet in the pool, feeling like my body, as usual, was a problem.

When we were almost through our beautiful week of massages, yoga, adventures, and bonding, my body was relaxed but my mind kept counting threats. I was shamefully counting the days we had left in Bali, on one hand dreading the return to normalcy and winter weather, on the other eager to return to familiar threats that I understood.

On the last day, we woke before the sun to chant and meditate. I let myself slip into a trance. My head swam and my body pulsed as I watched waves of inner undulations dance with the drumbeats. My body clenched and released as I breathed with purpose and depth, connecting to nothing but the entire inner universe. When I re-emerged on my mat in the yoga shala, the morning sun was bright, the cooks were cutting fruit in the kitchen, and something heavy weighed on my solar plexus.

The rest of the guests gathered to enjoy a technicolor breakfast of fresh fruit and dainty eggs, but I couldn't get comfortable. I wasn't hungry, I felt exhausted, my mind swam. The others noticed my empty plate and pained expression and bantered cheerfully about "Bali belly." If I was finally sick, I thought, I had just received what I accidentally prayed for in the silent, sweaty darkness of my bed. I poured myself a glass of ginger tea and padded barefoot across the lawn, away from the cheerful voices of the breakfast table and back to the cool darkness of my suite.

I tried to get a grip. I sat in the mosquito-netted fortress of the bed and let the crisp white sheets cool my lava-hot skin. My mind's eye flashed momentarily to the pill bottle in my kit bag, but I resisted. If I took one of those, I'd sleep through the whole day and miss out. I tried to breathe deeply, but the second attempt at a big inhale caught in my chest and emerged in a rib-crushing sob. The dam broke and a flood of emotion swelled from that heavy spot in the middle of my chest, rising up my throat and bursting out of my mouth in tearful gasps.

My travel companion walked in and stopped short when she saw me. I met her frightened gaze and tried to reassure her, but the words burst out in a howl.

"It's okay," I all-but-shouted, my voice booming off the high white walls of our suite, "I think I'm just releasing something." She backed out of the room and pulled the door shut. I heard the voices of the women sitting by the pool and tried not to think about what they might be saying. I felt like a lightweight, a buzzkill. *Who goes to paradise to freak out and cry?* I was wasting *everything*. Several shaking sobs later, a knock on the door told me the van was there to take me to my scheduled appointment with Jim, the healer.

"Fuck," I mumbled, scrambling out of bed to get composed. I was in no state to see some holy man. I was a wreck. I put on my brightest top, hoping it would distract from the pain seeping uncontrollably from me like floodwaters. On the ride over, I hugged myself against the air conditioning and watched the lush countryside pass by. Anger converged with my ever-present fear and I scolded myself for being in Bali and failing to enjoy every moment.

Jim didn't answer the bell right away and I stood on his palm-shaded patio, listening to a tinkling fountain and hoping he wouldn't be there and that I was off the hook. But after several minutes, I heard echoing footsteps and the big wooden door swung open. A man in his fifties gestured with a tanned, muscled arm, inviting me to enter. I sat in a chair in a corner of the stone cube where he conducted treatments, feeling tiny in the expansive space.

I had to push my voice to reach him across the room. "I don't know. I just get so stressed out. It feels like the world is trying to murder me."

"Royght. What else?"

"It's just this intense physical anxiety. I'm at the mercy of my body."

"Royght. And?

"Uh. And. It sucks? I'm exhausted! I'm living with the hand-brake on."

"I like your shirt."

"Oh, thank you." I pulled the thin cotton away from my body and noticed the electric watermelon color and how the armholes hung low to reveal a galaxy print bra underneath.

"Red. Root chakra. You picked that on purpose, y'know. Your body knows it needs to ground."

"Oh, great."

Jim invited me onto a massage table in the cavernous room so we could explore and rebalance my blockages. He was firm but kind, and I let myself cry, but only a little, because despite being truly exhausted and stressed, I wanted to impress him. And impressive women didn't snivel in strangers' homes.

I lay face-down on the table and felt his hands traverse various points in my body, where he squeezed and rubbed to break up the places where energy was blocked in my calves, my hips, my shoulders. He pinched my neck and

I felt it radiate and shoot goosebumps down my leg. He invited me to repeat mantras and hold my tongue to my upper palate to realign my chakras.

"You're concerned with how others perceive you." I thought about work and Koda and my Instagram feed. "Tell me what you'll do next time you think you need to gain another's approval."

"Press my tongue to the top of my mouth."

"Royght."

His assessment of my issues with fear, self-sabotage, and people-pleasing were accurate enough. They probably would have been for any thirty-something American woman who darkened his doorstep to cry on his table. Still, after going to doctor after doctor who treated my concerns with derision and my stomach pains with Ativan, it felt good to hear someone give actual answers. On the other end of the table, Jim's leather hands squeezed pressure points in my ankles as he explained how my relationship with my mother inhibited me from receiving pleasure. His Australian accent let the words run wild in the cement room; "Because of your mothahhhh. Hahd toyme with pleashaahhh." It was a new and strange feeling to be touched, and it felt safe to be seen in his stone jungle operating gallery. He recommended books about biofeedback with mantras to address the emotional root of physical ailments. He told me how the stress and distress I felt in my back, my jaw, my solar plexus, was all emotional. He told me that physically, I was *foyne*.

"Yeah, but, what if..." I thought, retreating into the familiar comfort of paranoia, then remembered I was in Bali and things manifested quickly here. I forgot my mission to remain composed. Co-mingled snot and tears ran down my nose and dripped through the face hole onto a woven mat below me. I was embarrassed by my puddle on his floor and I choked out some wisdom of my own.

"I think I need a tissue." He let go of my ankle and shoved a wad of Kleenex in front of my leaking face.

"I knew you needed one," he said. "But I needed you to ask for it."

He needed me to ask for it. This was a concept so foreign that I had to pass through customs before even trying it. I was so much, well, 'happier' isn't the word exactly, to shake in silence, to retreat from my retreat in dark, air-conditioned isolation, than ever ask for what I needed, because I never really knew.

The Volcano - Part II

The effects of the time in Bali didn't fully take hold until I got home.

Returning to Milwaukee from Bali in December was like being birthed into a new dimension. I traded juicy mangos and tropical jungle for icy wind and Christmas music at the grocery store. My family gathered at a cozy Italian place for a reunion dinner. The table was covered with a deep fried bounty of oversized dishes, hand-torn bread, and melted cheese. I nibbled on some antipasti and felt like an alien.

My rhythms were all off and I couldn't be sure I had re-entered reality or left it behind. After a week of eating fresh fruit, talking about soul purpose, and following bliss, I could barely understand when people talked about their petty problems at work or how they were negotiating with their arborist to take down the beetle-killed ash trees. *Which of these worlds was the real one, really?*

I woke up starving at 3am. My body had lost all concept of space and time. It just wanted a smoothie. But eventually the jet lag subsided and I got back into flow with that same old comfortable stress. I was back to work, back to wondering where I should move or travel to next. Back to stressing about money and how to save more and spend less and avoid debt but also cultivate a beautiful, stylish life. I was back to worrying about Koda, who was scheduled to go to the vet for the minor surgery that was supposed to address his lingering sinus issues.

He never recovered from the procedure. They found a malignant carcinoma when they went to intubate him for the sinus flush. They removed it, and sent him home with a cone around his head and a tentative prognosis.

Within a few days, he was lethargic and swollen. He would not eat. My dog, whose sworn enemy was Daylight Savings time because it pushed his dinner back an hour, suddenly turned his nose up to everything from kibble to savory bits of hamburger that I made just for him. That's how I knew it was the end. At the emergency clinic, a cold veterinarian nodded solemnly to confirm that it was time. It was the day before Christmas Eve when I made the choice to say goodbye to him forever.

I thanked her for taking me through the process with reassuring presence and most of all, certainty. She did not give me any maybes or false hopes. She gave me real answers and compassionate guidance. It was the most painful night of my life, but I knew it was real and the right thing to do, and there was comfort in knowing that the hardest action I ever took was also the most necessary. In a weird moment, Koda changed from my sweet but sick boy to a white pile on the floor under the blue fluorescence of the clinic lights.

That image brings me back to deep, bone-shaking sorrow, and I think it always will. It's the kind of grief that makes sense. It's easy to pinpoint and easy to understand. Real loss is obvious, like an explosion, and justified, and oddly comfortable because you know exactly why you're sad and can explain to anyone who asks and they will understand why a dog food commercial is making tears stream down your cheeks. Three weeks after we left Bali, Agung erupted and tens of thousands of residents were ordered to evacuate. They closed the airport and stranded tourists. The locals prayed and made offerings to the volcano. The effects of the eruption were real but temporary, and Bali rebuilt and life went on because living on the side of an active volcano means that sometimes your life shifts to handle a disaster.

Losing Koda was my eruption. Everyone who turned their eyes could see the billowing smoke and knew why people were fleeing their homes. But that rumbling sadness that twisted my stomach and erupted as stifled wails in a healer's house, or as deep fear when I shut off the lights at night; that was something else.

If love and death are the flashes that make the news, my grief that morning at Jim's was the pulsing magma under the surface. I could not point to it, I could not pick it up and show someone if they wanted to know why I was sad. It was just always there, threatening to blow, sending plumes of smoke into the sky to let off the pressure, but otherwise went unconsidered until Jim shifted a tectonic plate and let it burst upward where it could be seen. I always wanted to flee from it. But like the Balinese who refused to leave their homes as the earth trembled under their feet, I knew I could never outrun the eruption, because it was my home.

Secondhand

I kept traveling a lot. I didn't necessarily love it. I wasn't nursing some great passion for exotic cuisine or a penchant for historical sites. I did it because it was something to do. Moving around a lot as a kid instilled a certain level of wanderlust in me, and working a remote job now meant that if I saw something cool on Instagram, I could usually figure out a way to go there. So, I did. With each trip, I added to my stack of interesting anecdotes, but I wouldn't list "travel" as a hobby. My hobby was people.

Since I moved around a lot and didn't work in an office, I didn't have many deep friendships, and no real connection to a community. My main pipeline for fast interpersonal intimacy dried up when I quit drinking. I spent a lot of time alone. Luckily, I was learning to be good company.

Eventually though, my inspiration reserves got low and I needed to be among civilization for a while. So I traveled because nothing refueled the tank better than wandering around some new town like Jerome or Lisbon and just soaking in the newness. (I won't get into the obvious added benefit of expanding the geographical limits of your comfort zone. There's whole sections of the library dedicated to that.) I liked to walk the streets until some place like a bakery or a hat shop caught my eye, and I wandered in, and if I got the right vibe, started asking questions. *How long have you worked here? What shouldn't I miss while I'm in town? Is the town changing? Is that a good thing? Are these cupcakes gluten-free?*

Shopping provided a natural conversation starter, giving me the perfect "in" to develop microconnections with the world. I've spent hours chatting with locals in bead emporiums and coffee shops and gemstone museums. I would leave with renewed faith, reminded that interesting weirdos and their dogs abound, and all I had to do was let myself go say 'hi.' Being an outsider gave me the courage to engage. So, I heard about an event called "Divine Consign" which was a huge consignment sale, and I thought, *What the hell? I'll take the opportunity to be out in the world.*

Hot pink signs that said *Women's Sale Today! Gently Used Clothing for Women and Teens* wobbled on skinny metal posts in the frigid October wind. I followed them down a country road to a large modern church. I've shopped this event before. Sometimes, I found decent brands with the tags still on. Other times I got a headache from dusty stacks of fast fashion. It was kind of an adventure.

Inside, racks of secondhand denim and knits extended in every direction of what must have been the parish multipurpose room. The air smelled sickly sweet like those candles that make your house smell like you just made cinnamon rolls. A woman with a name tag rushed past me carrying a stack of clothes and started shoving hangers onto one of the racks. Looking back over her shoulder, she recited her line, "Just so you know, the pink stickers are half off."

Women pawed through the curated collection of pilling sweaters and once-worn dresses with furrowed brows. I started at the "Staff Picks" section that displayed higher-end items like Diane Von Furstenberg and Eileen Fisher and started my own stack of pieces that might fit into the inky black void of my winter wardrobe. The woman next to me wrestled a hanger out of a rack to get a closer look at a blouse and held it up in the air, "Sharon! Look at this! It's LOFT!"

Sharon placed a gently used Ugg boot back on a table and squinted, "Oh, I just love that neckline. Try it on!"

At one edge of the space, black fabric hung from metal piping that someone's handy husband probably fashioned into cubes for fitting rooms. A pre-teen ushered a line of waiting women into stalls as they opened up. Her ponytail swung wildly as she patrolled the stalls and expertly parroted customer service phrases, "Unfortunately we're all full right now. If you want to wait here, it'll just be a moment. Ma'am? Are you waiting to try on? This one's open. Follow me, please."

I follow her pendulum ponytail into a gauzy black box to try on my stack of someone else's unloved cashmere. Through the fabric walls I could clearly see people shopping out on the floor, and the women in the cube next to me who had doubled up for efficiency. They giggled and whooped when they found something they liked. "I need a sweater like this for the office! It gets so cold in there. And it's only seven bucks!"

My sweaters didn't work out, but I found a like-new leather jacket with a half-off sticker. *Score.* I wore it out of the box to where women in secondhand tunics and yoga pants walked a makeshift catwalk. They struck poses, tugged at clingy fabric, and glared at themselves in a large mirror leaning against the cinderblock wall. I walked past a dozen more women waiting their turn, and headed for the raised stage which served as the jewelry and name-brand bag showroom. I was looking for turquoise.

"Let me know if you want to see anything!" A volunteer across the table held up a small key and glanced with kohl-rimmed eyes at the glass-top boxes that kept semi-precious pieces separate from the costume jewels. She was around sixty, with icy silver bangs resting on the edge of black cat-eye glasses that magnified intense lilac eyes. A name tag pinned to her chest read "Shari."

"I'd love to check out this silver cuff," I pointed to one of the boxes, and she opened it up so I could start digging around.

I didn't look long before something even sparklier and more dynamic caught my eye. Behind Shari, a nymph of a woman paced and straightened jewelry in quick, catlike movements. Her name tag was covered in a layer of glitter and pink half-off stickers. Underneath, it said "Roxy."

Roxy disappeared from behind the table and appeared suddenly at my elbow, looking up at me with icy blue contact lenses. "That's Kendra Scott, you know," pointing at the gold chain in my hands.

"I don't know what that means," I lied, hoping to keep this elf woman talking.

"She's a designer. She has a store over at the Corners. She does a lot with drusies." She took the chain out of my hand and flipped it over to reveal a sparkly stone pendant.

"Ah, cool. Drusies." I repeated, placing the heavy necklace back in the glass-top box that Shari still held open for me.

"If you like anything we just have to put it in a bag with your name on it and take it to the front for you." I examined the collection of bangles and sterling earrings while Roxy and Shari chattered like birds on a wire. In unfinished bursts, they covered several topics at once. *It's been busy today. I can't believe it's so cold already! Kathy took a longer than usual break this morning and you know what that means.* (I didn't, but it was fun to speculate. Was Kathy a recovering addict sneaking hits in the church bathroom? Did she run off to meet her bad boy ex-lover at lunch? God, that is just so *classic Kathy*.)

They caught me listening and held me in their jewel-toned double gaze. A beaded bracelet slipped from my hands, which had started to sweat. I came clean, "I'm sorry, but you two are just so *chic*!" It was mostly true.

They were wrapped in head-to-toe black with accents of crescent moon patterns and layers of tulle. They each wore a headband, equally eye-catching but different to convey their individual spooky persuasion; one with velvety cat ears, the other a black veil that gave the wearer the aesthetic of a witchy bride. Shari wore lipstick so deeply blood-red it was almost black. Roxy's nails were leopard print decals.

"We are ready for Halloween!" they said, stating the obvious in perfect unison. "Plus both our birthdays are coming up. We get real into it."

"I dunno," I poked, "you ladies seem a little too nice to be Scorpios."

One thing I've learned on my travels is that a lighthearted astrology joke is a great way to find out if the people you're talking to are fun weirdos. If they're not, the joke shuts down the conversation and you can move on with your life. But sometimes instead you open a portal to deep personal revelations on the repurposed stage of a megachurch.

Roxy smiled and flitted away again while Shari shook her head. "No, no, no. I've got a tough side." Clearly a fun weirdo, she understood the reference to Scorpio types. Like their arachnid namesake, they are known to have a hard exoskeleton and a mean sting to protect a soft and squishy underbelly. "I had a tough life, so I had to get a tough side. I've got some fight in me."

"Mm-hmm," I narrowed my eyes and nodded in feigned disbelief.

"I don't let people push me. What do you do when people try to push you?"

"They wouldn't dare!" I joked.

I was putting on a show. I felt a kinship with these women because we shared a love for spooky fashion and consignment shopping, and now our conversation was going from zero to the-meaning-of-life thanks to one dumb joke. But I wasn't altogether lying. In fact, I felt like I was writing a character sketch for the woman I was trying to be, and she was so sure of herself and her worth that manipulative, shitty behavior didn't even register on her radar. Her bulletproof confidence shielded her so powerfully that people who tried her just withered and died. I attempted to channel her by conveying a touch of menace in a wide smile, and continued, "People know better than to push me. They want me on their side."

Shari stared, blinked her violet eyes, and inhaled. She saw right through me. "Now. See. You're going to walk away and I'm going to remember everything about you; your teeth, your hair, your nose ring. I spent my life having to see everything. I experienced a lot of trauma and now I can see and heal trauma with other people." She literally called me out for fronting. On a church stage, in front of God and the Coach bags.

I opened my eyes wide like a fawn and redirected, "Wait. Constantly noticing everything is a trauma thing?" She stared at me, nodded. She leaned forward in her chair, hovering over what was left of the sterling.

"Huh. I might have some work to do!" This was another stupid joke from a person who had been exposed to truckloads of therapy. My sketch had failed to recognize the deep inner work my character had already done to get here. I kept smiling though, showing Shari I was receptive.

"I had a tough time. I had to get strong. My father just tried to kill me again when he got Alzheimer's." She held her hands to her throat in a theatrical strangle while that word *again* echoed in my head. "But, I'm learning how to not take it on anymore. Now I can just put up my boundaries." She zipped up an invisible sweatshirt. "And oh boy, they don't like that," she said, gesturing toward her invisible antagonists somewhere over by the fitting rooms.

"Now I'm a practitioner in a program that helps people heal their trauma." Unprompted, she wrote the name of the group on a slip of paper and slid it into the bag with the turquoise and silver earrings I'd selected. At that moment, the authoritative tween from the fitting rooms bounded up to the table, looking fresh and out-of-context in the midst of this conversation. With the posture of a royal envoy, she asked Shari and Roxy, "Is there anything I can take to the front for you?" Shari handed her the ziploc with my jewels and the name of the trauma group and she scampered to the cash register. I'd pick it up when I checked out.

That was the thing with people and these interactions. Sometimes it was picked-over knits and gluten-free cupcakes. Sometimes it was intense micro-intimacy. But it was always people, so it was always interesting. Both the leather and the wisdom were someone else's first, but they were mine now.

The Fall

It was a steamy summer day in the lakeside city of Osh Kosh, Wisconsin. My hair was curled, my eyelashes were painted, and I felt like throwing up because I was with a group of people that just kept feeding me. My dress was stretched to its limits and the darts dug in where yet another meal of greasy local fare sat heavy in my stomach. I sucked in an inhalation and said a prayer of gratitude for the air conditioning in the black Escalade that shuttled us to the high school.

It was another night in a week of being transported like royalty from hotel to hometown diner to high school, and the other judges of the Miss Wisconsin pageant panted and sweated next to me in the leather seats. In a few minutes, we would file and smile to our seats at the front of the auditorium to dutifully judge the talents and toothy grins of the promising young participants. For this week, as our stomachs rumbled in testimony, our every need was catered to. We were to focus one hundred percent of our energy on identifying and selecting the most deserving young woman to reign as representative of The Badger State.

I was not a pageant girl. I felt the weight of the forty bobby pins in my professionally-curled coif. I tugged on my lace and my feet fought against the strappy shoes that imprisoned them. The friend who helped me pack, who sat in this Escalade and folding judge's chair before me, had scolded that I needed to "glam it up!" So, I strapped on the sparkliest spikes I could find in the DSW clearance room. Now my feet were in prison and my hands sat clasped on my satin lap so I wouldn't fidget and smear my lipstick. These were not the concerns of the women I was expected to scrutinize. They were trained in how to sit to avoid wrinkling their dresses. Their hair could hold a curl in 80% humidity. They swam in this tropical aquarium, and I felt like a catfish, plopped into their tank and asked to judge their colors.

I was not one to say "no" to an experience like this. When a friend grabbed me by the shoulders and told me she had a once-in-a-lifetime offer for me, I nearly agreed before I heard the specifics. Despite having exactly zero experience participating, attending, or even being aware of a pageant, she imagined I would be a perfect judge to take her place. I would stay in a beautiful bed-and-breakfast, she said. I'd get to dress up and meet interesting people. My experience as a professional in corporate America—and in technology no less—meant that I'd bring a unique perspective to the judging panel. *Why the hell not.*

I took a week off work, fished a paltry supply of dresses and heels from behind the trusty stack of denim in my closet, and drove two hours north from my parents' house to the shores of Lake Winnebago. Steam hovered above the corn in the fields, and banners for the pageant welcomed me to the idyllic brick facades of downtown Osh Kosh. The accommodations, as expected, were a tasteful bed-and-breakfast near town. I lined up my shoes and hung my dresses on a rack in a bathroom suited for a princess. Afternoon sunlight streamed in through stained glass windows, casting colorful shadows across a jacuzzi tub in the corner that occupied a space the size of a studio apartment.

No sooner had I unpacked and met my fellow judges when we were piled into our Escalade and taken to our first of what felt like thousands of meals. We were to taste the local cuisine, invited as guests of the proprietors to experience the finest that Osh Kosh could offer. In this part of Wisconsin, that meant Italian or fish fry. Another judge was a local Wisconsin girl. She lived near my family and had participated in pageants herself. The others were out-of-towners and pageant regulars. This was their first time judging Wisconsin, but just the latest in a long line of pageants. They did it for the love of the craft. They sewed rhinestones on dresses for friends, coached girls on their walks, and scrutinized personal platforms. At dinner, their cheeks got ruddy with wine and laughter as they exchanged raucous stories of bygone contestants, dress mishaps, and talent disasters.

"Y'all and I told her she needed to *sleep cute* if she wanted those curls to last another day, but did she listen?!"

"And would you believe there she was dancing to that SAME DAMN SONG another year!"

"Well you know she was fixin' to age out of the pageant and had to shine or say goodbye!"

This was their world, and I followed their lead as we began our proceedings. For two full days, we grilled the dozens of young hopefuls on their personal platforms, which ran the gamut from ending bullying to human trafficking awareness. They were written and packaged to express each woman's compassion and dedication to her cause.

After the boiling sun dipped below the cornfields, we glammed up and took our places at a long folding table in the orchestra of the auditorium and watched one charismatic, talented woman after another perform and pose. With immaculate hair and makeup and carefully fitted dresses, they performed choreography, showcased talents, and stood statuesque before our table in taped-on swimsuits to be scrutinized. I watched it all from my place below the stage, safely out of the spotlight. As they approached, I saw their legs shaking, waxed and stacked on platform heels. I thought *they are all so incredibly brave.*

For that week, I got to live a different life. I wore sparkly shoes and elegant outfits to embody the glamour of the event.

I attended welcome dinners with business leaders and representatives from the state capitol. I got to witness the next generation discuss what lights them up and what change they want to be in the world. But, when the pageant emcee called my name and invited me to introduce myself to a crowd of proud families, I was embarrassed. I was in that auditorium because I was invited by a friend who filled the role the previous year. For me, it was a glitzy vacation and a fun fish-out-of-water experience. I had not worked systematically through the pageant circuit and beat out less prepared women with my beauty, grace, and compassion to get here. So, I mentioned my high-tech job and my passion for yoga into the microphone, then handed it back and crumpled into my chair in a pile of satin, feeling ashamed.

The next night, the judges were invited onstage to perform in a crowd-pleasing pageant of our own. Prior to ascending the stairs, two of the other judges reminisced about a participant they watched throw up and pass out onstage. My ears began to ring. As we stepped into the limelight and I felt my stomach churn, I glanced into the wings for a trashcan, just in case.

Flashback

Months earlier, I was invited to speak onstage at a conference for work. It was a crowning moment in my career and I was prepared for it. I knew my speech backwards and forwards. As I delivered my talk, looking out over a crowd of potential clients and company bigwigs, I felt excited. But fifteen minutes into the session, something shifted. I was struck by a sudden wave of nausea. My head spun. I spent thirty more minutes pacing the stage, thinking I was about to puke. I kept talking and silently willing time to go faster. I contemplated pulling the fire alarm. At one point, I even removed my shoes.

That night, I collapsed onto my hotel bed. I replayed the scene of my catastrophic failure until I could muster the strength to catch a cab to meet up with some coworkers for dinner, where I pushed Thai fusion around on a plate for an hour and thought about curling up in bed.

The next day as I networked with a few attendees, they claimed not to have noticed anything weird about the session. We even landed some new business as a result of the presentation. Apparently, despite being in a hell of my own making, I had crushed my presentation, but I felt like a complete joke.

On the flight home I struck up a conversation with my seatmate. She was a nurse, and the conversation naturally floated to weird body stuff. I jovially expressed my frustration that human bodies don't come with an owner's manual, and shared how my stomach had begun to turn on me. I figured enough days had passed and I could share the tale as a funny anecdote, but her face dropped. She asked a few questions about the pain, and said it sounded like appendicitis. She even suggested I skip my connecting flight and head straight to urgent care. This led to yet another panic attack in the Denver airport. I found a medic who told me I was probably fine, gave me some Zofran, and sent me on my way, but not before joking about the inconvenience of a bursting appendix in a metal tube in the sky

By the time I got back to Wisconsin, I was reeling. Lord knows, I was accustomed to business trips going sideways from my time as a heavy celebratory drinker. Now that I'd quit the booze, I was *supposed* to be unstoppable! Panic was supposed to be a thing of the past. My health and habits were supposed to be bulletproof—I had worked so hard to get sidetracked by queasy, panicky vertigo. This could not stand. Still, I canceled my upcoming events and the wooziness persisted for years at a level that was enough to interrupt my life, but low enough that every doctor rolled their eyes and handed me a prescription for something calming. It led me down a winding path of diet changes, ab exercises, and breathing techniques to quell a deep and constant sense of dread.

Walking onstage that night at the pageant felt like returning to the scene of the crime. I was still terrified, but I took careful steps in my spike heels on the hardwood and proceeded to play-act my way through the experience. I even won the trivia contest for knowing that Osh Kosh was colloquially known as the "Event City" and "Osh Vegas." I was happy to win, but even happier that I hadn't swooned under the pressure or tripped on my dress and flashed an accidental boob. Though I was happy to be out of the lights, I also quietly enjoyed the rush.

We crowned a new Miss Wisconsin and I went back to my life of skinny jeans and conference calls, but I kept the glittery heels. They mostly stayed in their box in the closet, except for when my niece pulled them off the shelf to shuffle and sashay around the room like a "beautiful girl," as if the shoes had anything to do with that. I learned at the pageant that beauty queens were more about the queen than the beauty. Each of them was an example of a well-rounded and devoted young woman with vision, and yes, beauty too. The experience stuck with me as a source of inspiration to push myself past mediocrity toward becoming a woman that would hold up to my own judgment. *Could I walk across the stage in full view of everyone I knew and proudly state my name and what mattered most to me?* If not, I was betraying myself and the women at the pageant who deserved a judge who was at least half as accomplished as they were. I owed it to everyone to feel the fear, and do it anyway.

My niece sat in my lap at my desk, the sparkly pageant heels hanging by their straps from her ankles.

"Why do you love spooky stuff?" She pointed to a pencil holder in the shape of a skull that sat between astrology books and crystal geodes on my bookshelf.

"Spooky stuff?" I played dumb because I wanted to hear more from her wild five-year-old mind.

"Yeah. Spooky stuff. Like ghosts and skeletons and dead birds," she glanced toward the feathers hanging from a dream catcher on the far wall.

It was a good question, and one I was not prepared to answer. My own personal platform was built on being fun and light-hearted, but she was right. I did have an affinity for spooky stuff. My clothes were often black and my room dripped with witchy accoutrement, but her question caught me off guard because I didn't like scary stuff at all. I didn't handle fear well. My palms would sweat and my stomach would churn, as my brain held onto what scared me and wouldn't let it go. I took pains to avoid fear and squashed it when it showed up. Even dumb horror movies haunted my dreams for weeks. I wouldn't even watch the previews, because while I could laugh at the jump scares and spurting corn syrup in the moment, those shoddy monsters reappeared around bedtime, enhanced by the brutal realism of my imagination.

I have always been easily frightened. It started when I was a kid, spending a lot of time alone. In big, echoey houses, I was afraid of what might be in the closets and shadowy corners. Otherwise innocuous spaces like garages and basements were playgrounds for spiders and noxious ooze. Fear made every house feel haunted.

My brother and my dad and I watched movies together, and they usually got to pick. Usually it was something scary, and I sat with them because I would rather be scared and together than scared and alone. Afterward, I was haunted by memories of scary movie scenes—evil animals, brutal shootouts, snarling villains.

Even when we watched kid-friendly content like Disney, it wasn't much better. On the other side of every sparkly dress and serendipitous love story was early life trauma; a dead mother; an offer to sell your voice for a set of legs. Princesses were tormented by evil stepmothers who cast a black shadow over their idyllic memories of loving mothers they would never see again. Even Simba only became king after watching Mufasa brutally die, and getting blamed for it. My would-be heroes were symbols of resilience against odds that were stacked way, way against them. *Where were the tales of a well-adjusted kid happily taking over the family business and living a small but meaningful life?* Even kid-friendly content held the lesson that DEATH COMES FOR US ALL, but the movies drowned out the spooky silence of an empty house, so I learned again and again that life was about triumph over trauma. I began to believe that disaster lurked around every corner. My brother knew he could easily scare me, and took full advantage.

One of the houses we lived in had a bathroom with avocado-green carpeting, which matched the avocado-green bathtub. I loved it in there, because it made me feel like I was under the sea while I played with my mermaid Barbies until their hair got moldy. After my bath one dark afternoon, I walked back into my room and looked out the window where usually I could just see the shrubs and the sky. Instead of bushes, against the black backdrop of the winter sky, a gorilla stared back at me with evil red eyes. I ran into the kitchen frantically looking for someone to help me, but the adults were at work and the babysitter was splayed on a hot pink vinyl bean bag watching *Saved by the Bell.* The front door opened and my brother walked in, laughing and waving the gorilla mask.

After that, I started playing in the basement to avoid windows and red eyes. Even though I *knew* the gorilla wasn't real, I couldn't shake that queasy feeling that washed over me as I let my eyes focus on the darkness out the window, when I hoped to see shrub and sky but remembered those shiny red eyes and that toothy gorilla grimace. Even with its cold concrete and gurgling furnace, the basement felt like a safer bet.

My mom had brought a giant computer box home from her job, and I used crayons and safety scissors to turn it into a playhouse and gorilla-free sanctuary. I colored myself windows with flower boxes and a fireplace to keep me warm against the chill of the cinder block walls. But, the basement had its own risks. More than once, someone upstairs forgot about me and switched off the lights. I would emerge from the playhouse and whimper uselessly, fumbling toward the stairwell. My hands guided me through piles of toys toward the wall, where I felt cool metal that I thought might be the staircase handrail. I followed it, feeling cobwebs on my face as my shoes shuffled across the mystery grime on the concrete floor. When the lights blinked on and footsteps pounded down the stairs a few minutes later, my brother found me wedged between the furnace and the back wall, further than ever from safety. He rolled his eyes, flopped onto his waterbed, and powered up his Nintendo. I internalized the belief that everything good could become scary in an instant. For decades, panic continued to hit me swiftly like a switch was flipped and I was plunged into darkness. I fumbled through treatments and mitigation techniques and often ended up wedged between two maladaptive coping behaviors. I drank. I traveled. I hid. I overate (and underate). I worked too much. I shopped. Finally, I stopped. That's when healing happened. In the silence of stillness, I heard that the monster I was running from was the fear itself. And it was an inside job.

I think people who actually love being scared, God bless 'em, have a fundamental understanding that they are safe. They know that the scary thing on the screen can't actually hurt them. I never felt safe enough in my own skin to trust that the monsters would stay in the movies. I grew up in a series of houses haunted by sudden blackouts and gorilla infestations. I once found a pile of diamonds in the sunroom and then got scolded for collecting my treasure because I was actually playing with broken glass. I still haven't grown out of fear. I know because I put myself to the test by going through a high school haunted house. It ruined my life, at least a few months of it. The image of some shrimpy freshman menacingly riding a tricycle toward me in a Jigsaw mask shook me to my core and helped nightlight stocks soar. I still prefer to fall asleep with the TV on, because I prefer background noise to the sinister emptiness of silence. I don't think that makes me *not brave*, though. *Being brave isn't about not being scared, is it?* Being brave means feeling the fear and doing it anyway, like the girls who show up on stage, and like my niece, who has to practice being brave every day. I looked at her then.

"I guess I like spooky stuff because it lets me be friends with the stuff that scares me." I fiddled with some of the glittery crystals on my desk, and re-arranged a labradorite obelisk next to a pyrite disk. "Plus, it looks cool!"

She gave me an incredulous side-eye that said *Oh, Auntie* and suddenly seemed much older.

I pulled the skull from the shelf and held it in my hands as I considered her question. Spooky stuff. Like ghosts and skeletons. Like Halloween and the spooky impending darkness of winter. My late-September birthday means I always look forward to fall, even though there is something *spooky* about it. Nothing feels more achingly nostalgic to me than leaves swirling around golden corn stalks under blue-gray skies and a nip of chilly warning in the air. Even though it's the season that feels the most fleeting, reminding you most acutely of its inevitable end. Fall is the ultimate embodiment of the idea that death truly does come for us all.

After the pageant, I rented a house for the month of October and spent early mornings watching the white sun rise from the porch. Fat squirrels played chase under trees that swayed in a biting, northerly wind. The neighbor raked and raked and raked before disappearing behind his ramshackle shed and setting fire to his leafy haul. With each breeze, a million more bright yellow leaves fell and twirled mockingly onto his lawn.

The fragrant smoke from his bonfire rose to meet the tops of the towering oaks and maples. They so recently buzzed in that steamy summer haze, now they were one stiff gust away from being brittle and bare. Honking clouds of geese marked time in the sky as summer slid out of view and wintry Orion rose above the horizon with the harvest moon. To the not-so-distant west, heavy clouds gathered and threatened to dump a coat of snow on the hay bales and bring the brilliance to its final frozen end. No other season is so transparent in its transience.

The scarecrows can attest as they shiver in the gale, autumn is the only season that confronts us so directly with its impermanence. Technically no shorter than summer or winter, perhaps it's the only honest part of the year, the only season brave enough to demonstrate just how quickly it passes. It's a time that asks the courageous and contemplative to consider that the other seasons, and the years as well, pass just as quickly too.

While summer may be the payoff that we wait for all year, we forget to enjoy it while we nurse our sunburns. Winter soothes our dread with silvery snow sprinkles before brutalizing us with endless months of darkness. And everybody but the eager agronomist just waits and wishes for poor, sopping, stinking spring to be over. Isn't spring just the broccoli we choke down to get to summer's ice cream social?

But *fall*. Every gently falling leaf taps you on the shoulder and invites you to take a look around every now and then. The season's holidays force you to not only witness but celebrate the extremes of death and harvest and scarcity. Fall may be no shorter than summer, winter or spring, but it is the most contagiously self-aware, and it has helped me understand why I do love spooky stuff, after all. Death, like winter and fear itself, may be inevitable, but hiding won't prevent them. It's simply best to prepare, to hunker down and harvest your strength for the coming darkness.

It is in that spirit that I want to have tea with the crone in the clearing, and ask her about her birds and if she ever gets lonely or if she always enjoys the solitude and clear winter skies from her shack in the deep wild. It's in that spirit that I decided to accept the invitation to judge a beauty pageant despite being 10,000 leagues out of my depth. And it's in that spirit that I hold my niece's hand when she's scared during a sleepover so she knows that she can be scared and be brave, all at the same time. When I stand on my stage, even if my legs are shaking, I will share my authentic truth that I do like venturing into the darkness because that's where we find out what we're made of. That's where we fight our monsters. And when in doubt, all I needed to walk through my fear was a pair of sparkly shoes.

Homesick

Do you remember the first time you closed your eyes and drifted off to a completely other world? The first dream I remember involved my dad's red Nissan Pathfinder, a trip to the grocery store, and an alien.

In it, we drove down the sleepy streets of our Iowa town, and I felt her behind me. Strapped into my car seat, I squirmed to look. I peeked over the backseat and saw her sitting quietly, facing out the back window. I saw her sense me looking. Her slick green dreadlocks shivered and she turned her purple head to look up at me with enormous eyes. She stood up and I saw she was about my size—compact, with lanky limbs. I tensed when she reached a smooth purple arm toward me. Her veins glowed. She was calm, but I was afraid of her. She seemed like she could change at any moment.

I slammed my eyes shut, hiding from her. Her round green fingers touched down on my head and curiously explored my scalp, it sent shivers down my tiny spine. Then the car stopped. When we opened the back of the truck, there were only groceries. She was gone.

When I woke up, I still felt the shivers. My body was still taut from when I tensed against her touch. She never really went away. I felt her tap dance in my stomach and sit on my chest when I tried to sleep. I avoided her slithery whispers by keeping the TV or radio on. I didn't want to hear her inaudible chatter about danger, or feel her fingers poking me from the inside out. Sometimes she shook me like a hungry bear shakes a tree. She didn't seem to want me to relax. If I was stuck, she said, I was vulnerable. She told me there was danger in sitting still.

Her message was embedded in my cells even as I lost touch with the memory of her dream. I ran around with my eyes wide open and my heart slammed shut. I tensed when people touched me. Human closeness felt like something unseen brushing against your leg in murky water. If it wasn't me, I didn't want it. And after a long enough time of being afraid of what wasn't me, I became afraid of me, too.

I tried to outrun the fear, by burying my anxiety in adventure. I drove thousands of miles on self-imposed missions. For years, I crossed four states just to get a haircut because I liked my stylist in Colorado and appreciated that low level of chaos that came with constant travel. So every six months or so, when I needed a trim and a taste of mountain air, I embarked on a trip that turned a cut and color into a full-scale expedition.

Once, while I was sort of living part-time in Wisconsin, I woke up very early in the morning and left, fleeing not only boredom but also a polar vortex that had descended on the upper midwest and let the temperature plunge to a punishing forty below. A trip west was my easy and appealing escape, so I packed a lunchbox with snacks, queued up some podcasts, and settled in to let the miles roll by.

I had done this trip plenty of times before. Typically I took a decent chunk out of Nebraska then found a good-enough chain hotel because tired driving was said to be worse than drunk driving. I would eat packaged snacks for dinner to evade pathogenic truck stop food, drape my sleeping bag over the duvet to outsmart the bedbugs, and tuck into Netflix for a few hours of half sleep, then hit the road again at sunrise.

This time, I got cocky. I flew through the great Nebraskan expanse with plenty of sunlight and beef jerky to spare. With Odyssean hubris, I blew past my last opportunity for decent lodging and hurtled headlong into the horizon. I had no sooner passed the *Welcome to Colorful Colorado* sign when my car was engulfed by a roiling spring storm that obscured the lane lines with blowing snow and choked my wipers with frozen fog. My knuckles blanched on the steering wheel.

I was long past the homogenous but familiar comfort of La Quinta back in North Platte, so I followed the buzz of the snow-obscured neon to the next motel. The Platte Valley Budget Host was obliged to offer one-night-only access to a perfectly fine bed inside four cinder block walls. The room even came with a flyswatter. Despite the buzzing mini fridge and deserted lobby restaurant that advertised pizza but smelled like chow mein, the motel had its charm. My room had a view of the steel buffalo and tipi silhouettes of the Colorado Welcome Center, and I watched the slow progress of the snow plows as they trudged through the fog.

By the morning the storm had given way to a misty but navigable day. I knocked off the remaining three hours to Boulder and checked into my favorite hotel. The Boulderado offers beautifully appointed historic rooms and is also known to be haunted. I felt at home in the uniquely shaped guest rooms with ornate wallpaper and swoopy vintage furnishings. I got a kick out of stashing my clothes in a bureau instead of some particle board chest of drawers. I even got along with the ghosts, and the hotel sits at the center of a town that crawled with specters of my own past lives. From my perch at that corner window, I watched the rich tapestry of college town culture pass below and imagined my former selves among them on my way to work or, more likely, to the bar. If I listen closely I could hear the echoes of a thousand whiskey-fueled karaoke nights rising up from the bar downstairs. If I squinted I could imagine a projection of myself superimposed over Spruce Street, walking with a sway and a stolen sake glass.

I spent days living like a tourist in my former home, watching other people living and wondering if anyone had ever watched me. I didn't want to leave. After the snowstorm, the sun had come out and reminded me what it felt like to feel warm. I could not fathom returning to the deep freeze, so

I relocated to an AirBnb, tucked behind the first foothill a few minutes out of town.

The space was a sunny lower level with a sparse, woodsy vibe. I poured a whole day's worth of energy into settling in and making it my own. I got groceries and unpacked my salt lamp. I stacked books I brought on meditation on the bedside table. I set up my camp chair outside, facing the Rockies. When I was satisfied, I fixed a plate of loving snacks—olives, duck pâté, good cheese—and sat down for the first time in what felt like days. My body buzzed with the kinetic energy of days of fussing and running around. When I let myself be still, the buzzing subsided and something else emerged; a feeling, like a clenched fist, sitting squarely at my solar plexus. Something wasn't right. I checked the lock on the door, checked my car for forgotten groceries, checked my calendar for missed appointments. I found nothing. There was nothing wrong in the physical world, except for that this physical world, my temporary cabin home outfitted with the trappings of me to make it mine for the month, didn't actually feel like mine. I felt like an imposter. I felt homesick.

I was playing dress-up on a grand scale. I stepped into someone else's home to pretend it was mine, but my insides ached for something more permanent to cling to. I opened a window. The mountain air carried the scent of sunbaked pine needles into the space and I remembered hiking these mountains with my dog, Koda, and my friends from work. I remembered that commute east along that long, straight, congested road once I got my place in Denver. I remembered years of bouncing between the two cities trying every different combination of neighborhood and apartment and roommate and yoga studio and grocery store, looking for the Goldilocks scenario that unlocked that feeling of *home*. On paper, Colorado was everything I wanted. It was beautiful, progressive, outdoorsy. There was good food and smart people. I was never too far from a trailhead or a Whole Foods. But for almost ten years my feet never really touched the ground. I felt like a strong gust of wind could send me flying off the face of the earth at any moment.

My final attempt was a nice-enough one-bedroom downtown. It seemed to have everything I needed. It sat in a neighborhood straddling the expansive greenery of City Park and the buzzing neon of Colfax Avenue. If I choose to turn left, I could walk the dog along leafy avenues of historic homes with fit moms and their strollers. I could explore the city's museums or take in views of the skyline framed by the mountains at sunset. If I turned right, I could walk the longest street in the country and duck into diners and dive bars and communist bookstores. I had instant access to two worlds, and it still wasn't good enough.

But sitting in my rented cabin, thirty miles away from that old life, I clamored for something that felt familiar. It seemed like I should be able to pack my stuff and leave this stranger's house, drive downtown past the smelly dog food plant, pull into my parking spot, and climb the familiar stairs to my door. When I unlocked my door I would find Koda so happy to see me that his wagging tail would knock over the candles on the coffee table.

When rents in the city continued to skyrocket, I chose to leave my beige prison apartment. Then Koda never recovered from that surgery to remove his malignant carcinoma. So this feeling wasn't homesickness for that place, it was an ache to return to a life that no longer existed.

No wonder I loved my haunted hotel. Underneath all the travel and distractions, I was longing for a ghost.

The sun dipped behind the flatirons and I tried to shift the ache with some gratitude. I said a small prayer—*Thank you for the opportunity to step in and out of these physical and emotional spaces. I am grateful for my life.* The last rays of golden sunlight streamed through the windows. Magpies chattered a welcome from the pines. I was home enough, for now.

Brave Girls

I watched low clouds pour over the sandstone peaks of the Colorado Front Range from the window of my rented cabin. The gray damp lent itself to a productive day of work at my laptop, letting me get lost in deep projects or skim across my email inbox like a hawk across the glassy surface of an alpine lake. Sporadic to match the rainfall outside, every few hours my phone rang and I lost an hour to gossipy phone calls with other remote workers on my team. It was frenetic and pointless like a treadmill—I'd hang up and realize we hadn't accomplished anything in an hour. Around 5pm, the white winter sun dipped bleakly behind the foothills and my eyes would realize they were tired. I assembled a tray of snacks and collapsed in the awkward Ikea chair in front of the TV to devour a saved episode of Drag Race. This was my normal Friday night.

Icy raindrops ticked against the window as the sky darkened and I watched the drag queens pat their faces with elegant powder and wrap themselves in glamorous textures. Feathers, leather, gold lamé. I chased gluten-free crackers and salty Italian cheese with duck rillettes, and exhaled deeply to process another week.

My phone buzzed on the table, startling me and shaking the wrapper of the dark chocolate I was saving for dessert. The busy tableau of my iPhone revealed last-minute questions from work. Friends in a group chat confirming plans to meet for a hike in the morning. Pictures from my brother of his kids enjoying fish fry with our parents at their favorite Friday night dive. The whole family toasting the weekend with red cheeks and bourbon old fashioneds and fried lake perch, a thousand miles away. I responded with happy, hollow emojis and let the acrobatic drag queens soothe my feelings of isolation.

An hour later, another buzz. This time it was from Dad. The blue squares of text were inflated and bursting with energetic language. He had an eventful drive home. I skimmed the long text and keywords leapt off the screen. *Rolled stop sign. Breathalyzer.* Beads of sweat pooled above my eyebrows.

In his sleepy Wisconsin town peppered with supper clubs and boozy taverns, he rolled through an intersection on a Friday night in plain view of the local gendarme. Blue lights in his rearview precipitated a field sobriety test. His recent ankle surgery made the heel-toe walk impossible, but he was laughing it off. He had passed with a .03. The text glowed with defiant pride, *my eyes followed the cop's finger just fine.*

Christ. It was a dread-inducing account of a day-ruining event. I had had hundreds of nightmares about that exact scenario. I woke up sweating after imagining myself getting pulled over and tossed in some icy jail after bad judgment told me I could make it home after football Sunday at the bar. Behind the fear and the relief that Dad was okay was a quiet tug of vindication.

I could have seen this one coming. My father was no stranger to casual beers at lunch or running to the hardware store during a yard work intermission fueled by sunshine, hose water and Miller Lites. He never batted an eye about driving home after beers on the golf course bled into wine at dinner with the boys. He possessed a confidence around alcohol and his own tolerance that was distilled by a 1970's sixer-in-the-passenger-seat Midwest upbringing by an absentee father who was often traveling as a whiskey distributor, by the camaraderie he felt for an industry that had connected him to his wife when they met working for a beer distributorship in LA. He is the demographic that beer ads are made for, longing to be that solitary guy on a motorcycle on a wide-open highway, cracking open a cold one to celebrate his freedom. He bought the vision (and the neon sign) of buxom chicks delivering overflowing steins as heavy with ale as they are with coital symbolism.

So, what's a little buzzed driving to a man who was never indoctrinated by *Red Asphalt*, never traumatized by horror stories of beat cops wiping up brains next to an overturned jeep on prom night, like I was?

The ugly, averted possibilities played in my head in a made-for-TV kaleidoscope. His sunken eyes against the pallid cinder block wall as the bars slammed shut. Catching a shiv in the holding cell. Getting caught up with a record and letting the resentment fester and grow until he devolved into a disillusioned, disenfranchised serial offender. But no, this time he was lucky, divinely protected, and he knew it. The story ended with a proclamation—*I don't ever want to do that again.*

I breathed deep and paused the show, catching a queen flying midair into a death drop. The shitty Swedish chair dug into my back. I wondered timidly if this offered my lucky-and-reckless father an opportunity to reflect deeply and allow this experience to ripple like a pebble in a pond of self-awareness until it reached the peaceful shores of resolute, intentional living. God, I'd love that. I'd feel so proud and renewed, with a sour twist of told-ya-so. We would have something in common again, a similarity of steadfastness in reaction to close calls and lessons learned. I resisted the urge to call him and talk to him about how he felt, about the timing and the deeper meaning and his next steps. No, this wasn't the time. He could come to me if he wanted to talk big.

My phone vibrated once again against the empty snack plates and shook me back to life. My brother had weighed in on the family thread. "Take a deep breath and watch this," was the caption attached to a video of his four-year-old daughter onstage at the supper club that transformed to a honky tonk after the dinner rush. Standing next to the band, she was playing a tambourine in hot pink snow boots while tipsy women shuffled en masse before her like supplicant followers. Through a haze of green stage lighting, my niece tapped the tambourine against her thigh, lifting her giant blue eyes to the bandleader for reassurance.

A few weeks prior, before I packed my car and left Wisconsin in protest against the second polar vortex of the year, I hosted my brother's two kids for a sleepover. We built sleeping forts when the munchkins spent the night—one for each of them, in my room. We discovered this technique to be the most successful after several rounds of trial and error. Separate bedrooms were too spooky, the leather couch got too sweaty, the floor wasn't cozy enough, but Fort Finley and Norah Castle were comfortable, safe and effective. In tents made of blankets pinned on top of dressers with heavy dictionaries and chip clips, the kids were masters of their domain with nightlights, sound machines, stuffed animals, and layers of blankets.

The forts were custom-built to suit their inhabitants. Fort Finley reflected the resourceful seven-year-old future engineer inside. It was a labyrinthine cave between a bureau and the footboard of my bed with a system of doors and access points to keep his destructive sister out and a small travel alarm clock so he knew when it was time to wake me up in the morning. While Norah Castle, beautiful and wild like its namesake, was a breezy lean-to constructed with a floral tapestry from my college days. Inside, Norah enjoyed a tower of full-size air mattresses and a glowing unicorn night light.

Usually, this was a flawless system. But on this particular night, Norah was restless and resisted the comfort of her castle. She was violently overtired from a day of playing outside, not to mention cracked-out from a Grandma-sized scoop of ice cream and desperate for a sleep that she was afraid to succumb to. My usual tactics to help her weren't working. Again and again, I would tuck her in, give her a squeeze and reassure her that I was close by, but each time I'd try to walk away her little legs would kick the covers and she'd howl, "Noooooo, I'm just too scared!"

I was frustrated. I could hear her sleep-loving brother toss in his sleeping bag and groan in response to her cries. Plus, I wanted to sit down and mindlessly scroll Twitter after a long day of playing Super Auntie.

So we dismantled the walls of her castle so she could see me and know she was safe. But she watched me and protested every time I closed my eyes, breathlessly asking me not to go to sleep and leave her alone. She was just *too scared.*

I walked over and lay with her on the giant queen-sized monstrosity of an air mattress that dwarfed her. With a deep sigh, I opened a line of therapeutic questioning, asking first what she was scared of.

"I'm just too scared," she croaked, her voice hoarse from crying. I explained, matter-of-factly, that she was in a safe bed, in my safe room, in Grandma's safe house, in a safe town in the safe world, and that her big brother and the dog and I were right there with her. It was all so obvious, couldn't she see?

"Yeah, but I'm still too scared" was her whimpered reply. My jaw clenched. I needed to try something else. I rolled over and stared at her in feigned confrontation.

"You know what, girlfriend? I don't believe you." Her giant blueberry eyes stared at me, shocked, but curious. "Because I saw you today. I saw you skate across the frozen pond and mash bananas for pancakes with your bare hands. I saw you jump off a couch onto a half-inflated air mattress to launch your brother into the air. Those are not things that scared kids do! Those are brave things. So I think, actually, you're brave."

Delight rolled through my gut and out my mouth in a giggle. I was enjoying this line of thinking. I continued. "Actually! I remember when we went on a long hike through the snow all the way to the river and you got too close and slipped into the icy water. And I remember I asked if you could make it back home, and you stitched your brow and said 'yes' and walked all the way back with icy cold feet, like a champ! So I don't believe you. I know you're brave because I've seen it."

It was working. I paused while she stared at me. After a long minute, she whispered, "What other brave things did I do?"

I laughed, relieved, and reminded her of some of our better adventures. The dead raccoon we found in the woods after Finley got stuck in the mud and we had to pull him out of his boots to save him. The day we went to the buffalo farm to buy meat and let a chatty barn cat give us a tour. "Scared girls don't pet barn cats," I reminded her.

I stared at the ceiling, remembering, and noticed the sudden hush. I glanced over to see her eyes had closed and her breathing had slowed and a small, satisfied smile rested on her lips. I eased myself off the air mattress and tiptoed around Fort Finley back to my bed, where I skipped the Twitter scroll and slipped into sleep.

The next morning over yogurt and cereal she asked, "Hey Aunt Whee-Whee, what else do brave girls do?"

Icy sleet pelted the windows of the cabin and my iPhone buzzed in response. A new message from my sister-in-law, posted under the video of my brave girl and her tambourine.

"Norah explained to us on the drive home how the conversation will go when she tells you about her brave night. She said she was scared up there, but Whitney told her how scared people live. But not her! She's brave!"

Three dots on the screen signaled another message incoming.

"They miss you bunches. We all do."

I was improvising when I explained to Norah that scared people stay inside all day. That they don't have sleepovers or adventures on the farm, and only eat dry toast. If I'd been truly honest, I could have shared with her that scared people also endlessly scroll Twitter instead of making plans for their life. That scared people get addicted to work and stay in safe jobs and never write their novel. They stay in the town where their family lives because venturing off, knowing you'll be alone, makes you feel *just too scared*. Even if you know that you're driving in your safe car on the safe roads.

But that's not me, I'm brave! A week or two after the sleepover, I woke up on a Wednesday and drove from Milwaukee to Colorado with no set date to return. I got stuck in a snowstorm and had to sleep in my sleeping bag in a hotel room with a flyswatter on the wall. I kept going and made it to a cabin in the foothills where I enjoyed great snacks and good TV and I knew that family was always a text away.

I was brave because I did it even though I was scared, and because I could sit with all these feelings and cry and miss the munchkins, but also go for hikes up mountains and eat Vietnamese food and think about where to go next. And now, I was wondering if the always running was also something that scared people did when it was easier than making peace with a family that felt like it was growing in a different direction from you.

But I'm scared and I'm brave and soon enough I'll be on my own stage, just like Norah and her tambourine.

Chasers

I was in the cabin for three weeks. I went for early morning hikes, spent my days working, and evenings connecting with old friends, or more often, binge watching *Six Feet Under*. My time there was almost over and I woke up with a few days left with an unshakeable sense of dread. I had settled into my space. I made it my own, even cooked corned beef for the first time on the small stove. It had felt like a miniature lifetime. I couldn't shake this feeling that I had somehow wasted it.

I cozied up and hid inside my comfort-blanket habits. I was more committed to my distractions than to my experience. I was the Michelangelo of wasting time, and instead of painting the Sistine Chapel, I lay on my back waiting for my future to send me a text.

When I felt lonely, I turned on the TV or ran to the store for snacks. I silenced nagging voices with mundane errands that made me feel momentarily accomplished. I asked rhetorical questions—*Is turquoise jewelry cheaper at the pawn shops downtown or the rock shops in the mountains?*—and exhausted myself searching for the answers. I used busyness to cope with having a thousand options and no direction. I let life live me.

It was getting harder to ignore. I felt a sense of doom like an anvil sitting on my chest. It was pain like nuclear FOMO as I watched people live and continued to feel left out. The world felt like a beer commercial where everyone was having a blast, and I was the only one watching the TV. The dread wrapped icy fingers around my throat and I started to panic. *Was I dying?* I was out here, looking for home, failing. My thoughts raced. If I couldn't hack it here, in this familiar and perfect-on-paper place, I wouldn't ever feel at home. *Something's wrong.* My body responded. Tightened. My breath quickened and my head felt like a balloon about to burst. I thought about my family thousands of miles away. I thought about how all my old apartments had moved on and were occupied by other people now, probably people who knew what they were doing, with dogs that weren't dead. I wondered what would happen if I died in that cabin. My heart pounded faster when I understood that I could be blindsided at any moment by an aneurism or a mountain lion and they'd have to identify me by my dental records. My heart pounded thinking that out here on my own, my life could so easily be reduced to a recognizable set of teeth. I took a hard hike up Mt. Sanitas to help knock it loose. I took selfies against the expansive vistas for digital validation. When the likes stopped pouring in, the heavy feeling remained.

Manic, I paced around the cabin. The walls were closing in. I drove to the coffee shop to drown my unease with butter coffee and ginger shots. If I was about to collapse into oblivion, at least there would be people around.

That clenched fist in my gut whirred in time with the espresso machine. It said, *we gotta get out of here.* Outside, it was a chilly morning and the town was waking up. Shopkeepers opened their doors and their Open signs flickered to life. But this town was closed to me. I always felt like an outsider here. Smart, but not as smart as the entrepreneurs and engineers who stood in line at the sandwich place arguing about crypto and neural networks. Fit, but not as fit as the trail runners who bobbed from rock to rock along the ridge lines, their sinewy limbs glistening. Adventurous, but not as adventurous as the backcountry skiers or full-time psychics. I wanted to fit here, but my gut howled at the idea. As long as I was here, I would be unsettled. It could feel like an ulcer or allergic reaction or an empathic reaction to that homeless guy I saw poking through the dumpster. I could feel bored or hungry or completely unhinged. I rode the lizard brain thought spiral and considered the possibilities. I Googled "hard knot in stomach + heart palpitations." Google reminded me I was both dying and totally fine, which was true.

I wanted to make some "real changes." I wanted to meditate more. I wanted to feel connected. I wanted to get a kombucha and a manicure. I described, prescribed, assessed, treated, and made broad promises until I was exhausted and still paralyzed. I had run myself ragged avoiding fear and feelings again. I spent too much money in a manic round of modern retail hunt-and-gather. It left me feeling afraid, depleted, and disconnected, again. This was the ritual I was somehow most committed to, so there must be something comforting about the familiarity of the sweaty helpless fear of something so shapeless. I had nurtured this intimate relationship with anxiety for years, I must have held it dear. *If I let it go, what would be left?* I breathed into the knot, tried to connect with it like trying to connect with an earnestly barking dog.

What is it, girl?

I followed my feet to a bench overlooking the Flatirons jutting flatly into the azure sky. I tried to sit still but the waves of anxiety persisted. I wanted to be comfortable with a new kind of discomfort. I wanted to shift my stress into exhilaration, trade white knuckles for resilience, and control for trust. Maybe just decide that there was nothing wrong with me, and live accordingly.

Santa Fe was six hours away. I considered New Mexico and the myths I read about the Sandia Mountains. How the red desert seemed to straddle this world and others, how those mountains felt like portals to the stars. I let a vision of warm terra-cotta call me, and remembered that little alien from the backseat. I was so afraid of her. She was different and looked like something that the world wanted me to believe was dangerous. She seemed nothing like me until I stared at her and recognized her. I looked at her and she looked back. Looking into her globulous eyes meant confronting the infinite possibilities of my life.

I let her crawl into my lap and felt her soften. I softened, too. She wasn't the threat I thought she was. I didn't know where she came from, but she was a signal. If I didn't trust her, I couldn't trust anything. Hiding from her was hiding from my own potential. When I was brave enough to listen to her low-spoken murmurings, she reminded me that I could choose to not be in danger. I could become the danger to my enemies: complacency, stagnation, and ruin.

The danger, she whispered, was anything I wouldn't face. This world would confront me with what I hid from as long as I was hiding. It would grab me by the head and sink itself into me and kick and scream until I listened. *When I face the mystery of my life, it faces me back. We expand together.* I kept driving.

Topanga

In Sedona, a psychic told me I would write a book. From Arizona, I drove to Julian, California and got destroyed by ants and gluten, as you know. From Julian, I drove west and then north, trying on lives as I went. Mountains followed by beaches followed by some time spent in a yurt in a canyon. When I booked a week in a yurt, I was most skeptical about the concept of living in a circle. Would my space be divided into slices, like a pie? Would I have a sleeping slice, a working slice, and an eating slice? Would it feel weird and swirly in the yurt because there were no corners for energy to get stuck in?

I booked it anyway, reframing the skepticism into curiosity. I was spending the spring traveling around and trying on different types of lives. Before the yurt, I'd tried a condo on the beach, a casita in the desert, a cottage on a farm. Now, to really round out my experience, I was going to dabble in yurtlife in Topanga Canyon.

Yurts are the circular canvas tents made famous by the steppe-people of Mongolia, which appealed to me because it was kind of offbeat, and because the ancient Mongols possessed a number of qualities that I admired, like nomadism, eating local, and ruthlessness. Anyway, it was only a week. Uukhai!

I drove up a steep and windy road from the town of Topanga to find my yurt perched elegantly against a hillside, surrounded by tangled thickets and a soft carpet of wildflowers. I climbed a few steps onto a porch that was built into a wooden frame that surrounded the yurt and leaned against the railings to take in the sage-scented breeze. Lizards chased each other across fallen trees, and caterpillars scooted along the floorboards. So far, yurtlife was predictably idyllic.

My assumption about slices wasn't far off. The bed and bedside tables occupied about half the real estate, while the left-hand hemisphere was sliced into sections for a bathroom, a kitchen, and an area with a desk and a dining table.

I started settling in, pulling books off the bookshelf and reading snippets about the area. Turned out the main property the yurt sat on had hosted some raucous parties for offbeat Hollywood types back in the day. The sound of approaching footsteps caught my attention. Peeking out the front door, I was delighted to see an enormous dog had lumbered onto the porch. She was a giant, droopy thing with skin that hung from her bones like a sheet from a Scooby Doo ghost. Her giant, brown eyes gazed up at me questioningly and told me instantly that despite her monstrous proportions she was going to be a sweetheart.

I opened the door and she pushed past me determinedly to sniff the perimeter of the yurt and inspect my stack of suitcases. I sat in a small armchair and watched her. Satisfied with her nasal inspection, she loped over to me and set her bowling ball-sized head in my lap. Generous jowls left smears of drool on my jeans and she stared up at me expectantly. I scratched her floppy ears that were spread out on my leg and thanked her for the warm welcome.

"BALOOOOOO!" came a shout from the main house, and I heard movement on the stone path connecting the yurt to the rest of the compound. I heard them climb the steps and a small man stood framed in the miniature French doors. "Oh gosh, I'm so sorry. She's friendly."

"Oh, thank goodness!" I responded, tilting my head toward the smears of slobber on my leg, grinning to convey my legitimate unbotheredness. We exchanged introductions and my host offered to give me a tour. I glanced around the yurt, confused. I had it pretty well figured out already.

"I mean, outside! There's a lot to see!" I followed him to the porch, down the stairs and to a gate in a small wire fence. Next to the gate hung a sign with big block letters, rainbow paint chipped and faded over decades: ROCK WORLD.

Traversing a landscape of stacked and scattered boulders, my host showed off his local knowledge, pointing out and naming local plants, stopping to pick grasses, handing me a stem before popping one in his mouth. "It's wild mustard, try some! It's great in a salad." He stared at me, eyes darting between the weed and my face, imploring me silently to eat it. I hesitated, imagining Baloo and her canyon dog friends poking through these same fields, casually lifting a leg on the grasses I was being invited to ingest. He was still staring. I ate the leaf. Satisfied, he turned his back and continued upwards toward the apex of ROCK WORLD. I clawed the bitter green goo off my tongue, forgoing the immersive foraging experience. I doubted I'd ever be brave enough to consume a plant handed to me in a field by some eager stranger. We climbed to the top of a stack of rocks and looked north over the canyon. The sun was beginning to sink behind the mountains toward the ocean, and a thin layer of fog was pouring over the top of the hills. It was breathtaking.

"Let me know if there is anything else you need." My brave, leaf-munching host dropped me off back at the yurt and walked to the main house, Baloo padding heavily beside him.

In the twilight, the yurt got even cuter. Tasteful lamps lit the circular space in a golden glow that played off the solid wood beams along the ceiling. I spent some time writing, counting my blessings, and smelling the sweet breeze wafting in through the open window zippers.

An owl hooted nearby and cut through the encroaching quiet. Baloo answered swiftly with a big bark that echoed from her barrel chest, closer than I would have expected. She had wandered back to the yurt and claimed a post on the wooden frame outside, sniffing out over the canyon and adding her voice to the cacophony. Now that I knew she was there, I could suddenly hear her heavy breathing through the canvas. I walked to the door with the intention of joining her in the twilight howl.

The switch for the porchlight was right at eye level. I squinted at what I thought might be an extra button on top of the light switch. When my eyes adjusted, I saw it was a spider, the size of a nickel, balancing on the wiring and daring me to bring my meaty hand down anywhere near her domain.

I grabbed a mason jar and a magazine and detained this intruder. I escorted her to a potted succulent on the porch, feeling very proud of my bravery and the kindness I was showing to the eight-legged locals by ignoring my instinct to scream and smash her at first sight. As I stood on the porch, basking in my own benevolence under the purple California sky, I watched her navigate from the succulent to the soil. She rappelled deftly down the side of the terra cotta, back to the wooden beams of the porch, then waltzed pointedly up the frame of the door and through the tiniest tear in the canvas, entering the yurt at the exact spot I had found her.

I instantly understood my place in yurtworld. It was her hillside, I was just glamping in it. So I spoke to her, hoping to broker a treaty.

"Okay girlfriend, I get it. This is your spot. I don't want to mess with you. I am happy to coexist here if we can agree on the terms. If you can pledge not to rappel down your web into my mouth while I'm sleeping, then I will keep my cool when I see you and keep my rolled up newspaper stashed. Do we have a deal?"

She sat stoic on the light switch. I put faith in the power of my intention, and hoped she wasn't the type to lay eggs in human crevices.

For the next week, I lived and worked in the yurt. I adjusted to the fact that the kitchen sink was directly next to the toilet, because in yurtworld, the water is where it is, so all things that require water are clumped together. I learned to just gently turn my back as I washed my coffee mugs, pretending the toilet wasn't there.

I drank my coffee on the porch, listening to the birdsong and catching whiffs of ocean mist that spilled over the mountains. As far as I could tell, the spider was keeping her promise. I usually saw her perched in her spot on the light switch. Sometimes she climbed a beam to her pied-à-terre on the ceiling.

I broke up my days with drives into town, hikes to lookout points, and popping down the canyon to dip my toes in the ocean. One night I followed some backroads down to Malibu to catch the sunset, at which point I learned that Malibu faces south and was not the ideal venue for sunset watching that I had imagined. (Travel is all about learning.)

Even the internet connection up there was pretty decent, so I could keep working uninterrupted. Cell connection was trickier, but I discovered the best service happened from the center of the yurt circle, so I laid in the middle of the bed with my head hanging off the end to take my conference calls. I strategized with my coworkers and gazed out the porthole in the roof where the beams came together. The light would change as the day wore on and I would take a minute to be thankful for this pleasant experience in almost-nature.

Midway through my week, the view from my bed began to change. Shiny ceiling beams started showing signs of life. Gauzy webs hung from the highest reaches near the porthole, connecting to small webbed encampments built against the canvas. In real time, I watched as my spider sister's cohort maneuvered and machinated, colonizing the roof space with their webs.

"I hope our agreement still stands," I said out loud, and the spiders continued to build above my head, telling me in no uncertain terms whose yurt this was, really. I could swiffer all I liked, they seemed to say, I could hit those beams with an extender-arm duster as much as I wanted to, but like a bad penny, they would come back. I was on borrowed time here, they said. This canyon was a wild place for wild creatures.

The spiders were a force as inevitable as the tide or the sunrise, mirroring the persistent wildness of the canyon. A year without those spiders and the bug population would grow out of control. The bats would get complacent, the lizards obese. The whole system would be desperately out of whack. A year without people, though, and the canyon would just return to a lush coastal jungle, finding a natural order of spiders, wild mustard, geckos, and sage. Baloo and her gang would live off trash and wild turkeys without a second thought.

I knew who the real intruder was.

Topanga - Part II

My nomadic tendencies were motivated by a search for a place that felt like home, that I also problematically didn't believe existed. When people asked me that fundamental question about where I'm from, hoping for a quick and relatable answer, I usually sigh and shake my head and try to gauge how long they might be willing to listen to me ramble about a childhood of school changes at the hands of corporate America which gave way to a drifting adulthood, empowered by the tech boom's always-on connectivity and AirBnb. Sometimes I'll say "all over" and be done with it.

More often, a conversation begins that ends with me sputtering excuses about not knowing where to settle down, and I'll feel frustrated and annoyed with myself for talking so much in response to a question that deserves a short answer. Detroit. Bay Area. A shipping container in a vacant lot behind Family Dollar. That's what people want to hear, after all, not some angsty diatribe about the Rat Park experiment, rising rents in our urban centers, or the feeling of disconnection that comes with the territory of our globalized society. People seem to want something with defined edges and all I can give them is a cloudy wisp of a story.

But this time I was intentionally traveling to artsy weirdo hotspots like Sedona and Julian to see if artsy weirdos were my people. Short answer—yes. Longer answer—yes with several conditions. I was paying attention, this time around, to how a place informs culture, especially with regards to geography and how it models lifestyles, naturally molding inhabitants into reflections of itself. Case in point: a dusty climber loping roadside with a bulky crash pad strapped to his back blends in like a mule deer in the Rockies, but drop him in the middle of Chicago, and he's as alien as a luchador at high tea.

I was, for many years, a willing participant in this kind of geographical assimilation. Living in Boulder turned me into a kale-craving vegetarian who cycled to hot yoga and lived in service to preserving the sanctity of 'the bubble.' When I moved to places like Cleveland and Milwaukee, the habits that served as camouflage in a front range hippie outpost rendered me a notable weirdo, so I adapted and adjusted and found a permutation of my unshakeable values like health, wealth, and outdoorsiness that aligned with whatever place I was in at the time. In Cleveland I got good at golf and jumped on the Cavaliers bandwagon. In Milwaukee I found the craftspeople who made furniture from barn doors and got interested in farming.

A lifetime of moving around developed—or at least revealed—an infinite adaptability that led me to believe I could feasibly move anywhere (within reason) and be fine. But as an adult with agency and an affinity for kombucha and grass-fed ribeye, I traveled in search of a place with values and resources that would nurture the best possible version of myself, which was healthy, hard at work, attuned to nature, and connected to community.

Life as a cultural chameleon was fun and the stories abounded, but a quiet nag at the back of my brain reminded me that one day, when someone asks me where I'm from, I want to be able to say "I'm from here."

I could have gone to any number of places, but most places just didn't feel quite right, and I was starting to understand why I felt alienated even in the places that catered to people like me. Within every cultural community that I tried to drop into, there existed a spectrum of both tolerance (insiders' acceptance of outsiders) and tolerability (outsiders' ability to deal with insider quirks).

On each far end of every subculture lived the try-hards and true-believers, while somewhere in the middle, you could find the normal heart-centered few who lived but didn't die by the lifestyle. (Shout out to these fellow normal weirdos.) But given too much isolation and not enough stress-testing, a community could reach a level of oblivious sanctimony that is fascinating in small doses and infuriating over time.

I drove to Topanga down a steep, winding road to get a taste of the local scene. I found a little cafe that, in addition to coffee and pastries, showcased local artisan products like patchouli skin serums and gemstone jewelry. But the real focal point were the patrons: a milieu of locals unknowingly participating in a parade of long dead and dying subcultures.

I paid for my coffee and some vintage postcards and sat down to pen some notes to my niece and nephew. In the small, damp courtyard I watched like a wildlife biologist as an all-you-can-judge buffet of expired coolness held court across the bubbling koi pond. The white fibers of an elder hippie's Gandalf beard had begun to interweave with his baja hoodie. A geriatric rocker in double denim pontificated on spacetime for a young viking and a lithe fur-clad ingenue.

In five minutes, their conversation leapt like jazz notes from geopolitics to the American exodus, Norse mythology, and the perks of life in the jungle. Under the surface of each of these disparate topics, a stealth but very present grasping for validation. 'Please, see that I am not only smart, but also edgy' implored each enthusiastic endorsement of the gray-haired rockstar's pronouncements. Even when they were just talking about movies.

"Loki would obviously win in a fight, because Thor's moral principles would be his downfall."

"The real myths were way darker than the Marvel interpretations, and thus much more realistic. Modern audiences couldn't handle them."

The hippie, the groupie, the young viking, and the rock-and-roller all agreed it was worth getting out of the country by 2020. An unspoken understanding underpinned their conversation. This country in which they sipped cheap coffee in a rustic luxe courtyard, pontificating freely on politics and history, was going to hell.

Each of them weighed in on their exit strategy. This handful of free spirits, aggressively unencumbered by any societal push toward conformity, all in perfect agreement. Not just on politics, but on the inevitability of space travel.

If given the chance they'd obviously do nothing but traverse the galaxy looking for new planets. They spoke with a colonizer's confidence, treating survival as some grand adventure as if they were not the type of people rendered sweaty and flustered by the slightest inconvenience. As if they had not been spoon-fed ideas and identity by a plush first-world life. Their experience was so good that they believed it had been hard-won, and that they could win it again. But their soft hands betrayed them. Or so I believed, judging from two bistro tables over, doing the same damn thing.

They spoke of actual existential threats like hurtling through the vacuum of space with the casual demeanor of someone who had done it not once but routinely, with the confidence of someone who knew in some distant world, a sweetly compliant alien princess waited millennia for a coddled and hairless earthling to blow the gel sac where she kept her mind with half-remembered Jim Morrison lyrics.

Of course, this was all a complete projection of my own fear of fragility, and doubts about my own authenticity and self-sufficiency. Through the lens of my own sweet, sheltered life, I perceived posturing from the weak-willed as a confrontation, as if they were mocking me. I liked to believe I had what it took, perhaps not to hurtle through space but certainly to decide wisely not to. But I've lived as lucky and coddled a life as anyone. The safety that I had experienced had been given to me; I was fooling myself if I thought I had earned it.

So, I finished my postcards and applied desert flower forever stamps before dropping them into a mailbox. My little ones would receive them and maybe they'd believe their auntie was adventurous, or maybe they'd just want me to come home. They could've cared less if I was living authentically, if I was cool or brave or interesting. They just wanted me to come over and build forts with them. Perhaps by traveling and searching for my home, like that aging hippie arguing with the grizzled rocker about whether or not Jim Morrison truly embraced his dark side or was just posing for the fandom, I too, was missing the point entirely.

First Impressions

Back in Wisconsin, I watched my bank account refill at the same pace that my soul drained from wanderlust and that pervasive feeling of stuckness. I made a compromise. One more adventure. I wouldn't go crazy. Nowhere too far or wild to destabilize the sudden inkling of resolve I had about slowing down. I found a retreat outside of Asheville, North Carolina. It was tucked in the Appalachian forest and promised a week of yoga, hiking, and community fueled by homemade gluten-free cuisine. It was priced right and set to begin in just a few weeks. My nervous system remained attuned to changing landscapes. One final push of excitement was just what I needed before settling into Wisconsin for the holidays.

I drove south, giving Chicago an irrationally wide berth to avoid the stress of city traffic, because I still got shaky in situations where I felt stuck. And if anything could make me feel stuck, it was ten lanes of angry Chicagoans. Instead, I sped through bleak rural wind farms while a light snow fell. From southern Indiana I crossed the river into Kentucky as it was getting dark and found a spot to settle in for the night outside of Lexington. When I woke up, a freak storm had dumped four inches of snow and gummed up the highways. I asked for a late checkout and settled in, working from my laptop and watching reruns of The Office on the hotel TV.

By noon, the roads and the sky cleared and I headed out and into the mountains. The clouds were exceptionally low, and as I climbed in elevation

I was soon completely engulfed in dense fog. Visibility barely reached beyond the hood of my car. With semi trucks on either side of me through the twisty mountain passes, I slowed down, breathed deep, and nosed my way through. The fog cleared near Rocky Top and I pulled off to get gas. My hands were claws on the steering wheel and my ears rang as I killed the engine. I took a deep breath and screamed as loudly as I could. After thirty miles of treacherous fog, I needed to purge some adrenaline. It helped.

Dropping into North Carolina, the views opened up to reveal misty forests and waterfalls gushing from rocky roadside springs. Once in town, I pulled into a city park to stretch my legs and call my dad.

"It's pretty cool here!" I told him, casually. He was well-acquainted with my ongoing saga to find a home. I had asked him once to describe my life in a word and he chose "turbulent," which was ironic because he was the one who was always down for a midnight road trip to Yosemite and therefore held at least part of the blame. I heard wanderlust, tinged with a dusting of envy, in his voice.

"You may be onto something down there, BBG. That whole mid-Atlantic mountain region might have something going on."

I told him I'd keep him posted and hung up. I felt something tugging from within. It didn't feel like normal anxiety, I didn't feel the urge to seek a port-a-potty. There was a call to this place. There was something about how the fog clung to the red leaf tree tops and the mountains that rolled gently in every direction. They were present and un-intimidating without the braggadocious scale of the Rockies. They were older and felt calmer. Something about them made me feel held. There was something familiar in the scent of wet leaves and rich earth.

I spent a few days in an AirBnb on the west side of the city, exploring. I made rings with a silversmith in the River Arts District and sipped coffee on the banks of the French Broad. I liked the old growth forest and abundance of water. I liked how the people at the grocery store would stop to talk to each other. Nobody was in much of a hurry. I liked how nothing was in a grid. It had a sense of place. I knew exactly, unequivocally where I was.

The retreat was in a large home tucked into the mountains east of town. It was November and the mornings were crisp with an overlay of clouds above the fiery trees. I came here following a call that did not have a clear message. I had followed it, curious and unsure. I was about to dabble in a level of vulnerability that felt more dangerous than a hundred solo road trips.

Werewolf

A guru leading a sister circle for the retreat stared into my eyes and said, "Self-love is a power play." She nodded with crystal conviction and looked around the circle, stopping at each of us to make intense eye contact and offer a reassuring moment of acknowledgment. We sat on the floor of the basement of a vacation home outside of town, holding hands and nodding back at the leader of this ceremony, in which we were stepping into some unknown but purpose-driven future. Before we could transcend, she told us, we had to cut the cords of everything that held us back.

Together, we chanted "I love you, I'm sorry. Please forgive me. Thank you," over and over, in harmony that bounced like the candlelight across the walls. The mantra went down like whiskey, smooth at first but with a wild turn, unlocking some deep inner ache that burst out of my chest in sobs and gobs of snot. I thought of the people I was angry with.

One face shifted to the next in a twisted slideshow of rejection and betrayal. I saw judgy sneers and snotty emails and remembered a recurring nightmare where I screamed and screamed at people who refused to hear me. I saw myself in the center of a sacrificial circle, twisting to make myself smaller as a cackling crowd hurled invisible arrows that sank deep into my skin.

I kept singing and the slideshow dissolved, leaving one lone figure hulking and masked in a shadow that spread over my bruised and tender form. I shifted my focus and saw a familiar face that I despised more than any other.

It was the face of that person who taught me that rejection is a birthright, and betrayal is a certainty. It was me. Like a horror movie, the call was coming from inside the house.

No one could ever hurt me as badly as I hurt myself. Sometime long ago I decided that owning my pain was safe, maybe even brave. It felt like owning my power, holding it tightly so it was under my control. I had thrown a harness on a wild animal and now I had it cornered and it was freaking out, snarling and snapping at me in fearful revolt.

I inhaled the palo santo smoke that hung in the air and released my neighbor's hand, reaching for a tissue box to wipe the tears that streamed down my cheeks. I hid my face and thought about all the ways I chose to torture myself, like with a dialogue of inner critique that was Wintour-esque in its cutting precision, a profound misdirection of tenacity and discernment toward identifying every imperfection. I considered the time and precious brain cells spent ideating, crafting, and salving self-inflicted wounds to inoculate against rejection.

It was self-harm in the disguise of self-preservation; a wolf in luxe lambswool.

The chanting faded out in soft tones. Around the circle, women sat peacefully with closed eyes, slight smiles on their lips. I tried to disappear into the wall. Our guide's aquamarine eyes made their way around the circle and locked onto me and I felt the sobs climbing out of my chest again. I scowled and shook my head, burying my face in my knees, trying to swallow the outburst. I wanted to run outside, deep into the woods, rip off my shirt, and howl through my tears at the full moon like a werewolf. Out there, I could let it run its course, and limp back to town later in bloodstained tatters, hang my head and apologize for the destruction I caused by having these messy feelings.

Instead, I tapped into years of trained restraint and stopped the flow. The shame of vulnerability wrapped around me like latex, sterile and confining. I figured maybe I could tap back into the tears later when I was alone. When it was safe.

Crying in front of other people felt tiresome and rude. Not to mention the inevitable shift of power that comes from revealing yourself to others. Now, at any moment these sisters and friends could throw those tears right back at me, call me out for being weak, decide I wasn't worth the effort. And I would be alone again, having trusted someone who could not be trusted, letting the wolf guard the flock. Three slow, deep breaths, and the tears gave way to hyena laughter that poured out of me in desperate yelps.

All of this, because of an invitation to forgive, and the sudden knowing that the only one judging me for having feelings was me.

Perhaps, I thought, as I glanced around the circle and saw so many sets of warm, welcoming, understanding eyes, it wasn't actually brave to hide behind spiky shields of aloof detachment, holding a knife to my own throat and threatening that I was just crazy enough to slice. But getting right with being seen meant being okay with sitting with myself. It meant identifying and cutting out my delusions, noticing and ditching the excuses, seeing the person holding me back for who she really was.

This felt big.

Had I discovered some key to life? I felt triumphant like an explorer unearthing an undiscovered shipwreck, although it was just the sunken ruins of my own potential for emotional connection. Still, I wanted to ride through town on horseback and alert the villagers: *get right with yourself, people! Know the real enemy!*

But the truths that get revealed through mystical moments of divine self-discovery, even when they feel so poignant and universal, sound forced and insane out of context. I can't turn to the person behind me in line at Whole Foods and ask them when was the last time they let themselves truly feel, right?

No, trying to share the magic secrets of my own shipwreck with someone who wasn't there was like talking into the receiver on a prison visitation phone. You could scream all you like but nothing was getting through unless the other person picked up the receiver, too. Just like the judgment started with me, so did the salvation. The monsters that haunted me were always a projection. And the people I was intended to *save* were me, myself, and I. By healing, I tamed that werewolf, stopped the circus. Self-love was the power play that was not selfish, but sovereign.

I wondered what would actually happen if I let myself be messy. What if my house got gross and my hair wasn't clean? What if I ate pumpkin pie for breakfast a couple days in a row? The deepest fear was that the world would reject me, that I'd be catapulted into space for failing to adhere to the standards we set and agreed upon, and friends and family would second-guess their association with me.

On the other hand, slipping meant fighting an uphill battle to get back to good standing. Re-raveling those parts that came unraveled would be a grueling process. There would be apologies to make. Unless, the act of trying felt different when it was an accepted part of the natural order. What really happened is that I discovered that the "together" version of me would always be there, because she is as much me as any other permutation of my identity on any given day. She's just as much *me* as this messy bun slob in sweats who goes out for coffee without makeup and cries at commercials. You'll always be able to tap back into her coiffed hair and clean skin and carefully selected attire, when you're good and ready.

Effort was the thing I valued above all else when it came to work and style and achievement, but it felt different when borne out of the depths of my inner knowing. I was learning to appreciate the messy girl who actually wanted to try something, even to the horror of my former self who, without irony, was trying so hard at every moment that she didn't even realize it. So hell, I gave it a shot. I got it together by falling apart.

Asheville

I was still technically intentionally homeless on St. Patrick's Day 2020. I was in Phoenix, Arizona for a wedding. We didn't know it was the last wedding before the pandemic brought events and normalcy to a screeching halt. As the world shut down, I took my last flight back to Wisconsin.

The world was under lockdown. I was relieved to be in the relative comfort of my parents' house, where there was plenty of space and toilet paper, and I was afraid of getting stuck there forever. I wished I had a home of my own to shelter in while the world went crazy. I wondered what other people were doing and reached out to the sister circle guru from the Asheville yoga retreat, Krissy. I had bought some pendants from her and given her the link to my blog. We had stayed in touch. She was new to Asheville and working on cultivating community. I wondered if it was different in Asheville. We talked on the phone. She shared that she and her husband had purchased a house and were planning to use the basement as an AirBnb. She said those plans felt foiled by the news, but otherwise she was happy to be stuck in a place that felt full of friends and access to the safety of nature. Her words were loud, and stirred that sense of longing for home. She heard me sigh.

"What about you, what's your plan?"

"I don't know. I really don't. I knew I was getting close to the end of my travels, but I didn't expect to get grounded so literally. I really hope I'm not stuck in Wisconsin forever."

"Where else could you be?"

"The answer to that used to be literally anywhere. Now? I'm not so sure. It seems like everywhere on the planet is having the same experience. Everywhere is locked down. I don't know where there is to go. If this is going to be a thing, I just want to be with good people. I won't mind being stuck if the stuck-ness is an opportunity to settle in. I actually wouldn't mind some time to settle in, be quiet, work on creative projects."

"It sounds like you're craving community. Would you ever consider coming back down here?"

"Honestly? Hell yeah. There is something super special about Asheville."

"Well, maybe you should just come here. You could stay in our basement. Obviously the AirBnb isn't going to be a thing until this all blows over. You'd be welcome."

It was the invitation I had been waiting for, but I was wary. I felt like a stray dog being invited into a home for the first time. It seemed like it might be warm in there. It smelled good. They seemed nice, but it could also be a trap.

"Seriously? What would that look like? Are you saying I could stick around a couple of days, or until this thing blows over?"

"We can play it by ear. We wouldn't make you sign a lease. I know you don't want to get tied down. But it might be a nice way to wait out the lockdown before you hit the road again." The warm invitation with no strings attached felt too good to be true. My mind reeled. "Listen. It seems like we're all going into a quarantine. Do you want to quarantine with your parents in Wisconsin?"

I didn't. Being in my parents' home was just another beautiful prison. I was comfortable. The food was good, and there was no opportunity for up-leveling. I had no community there. The sound healings at the taxidermy house were my only social outlet. I was a fish out of water in a small town where everyone else knew one another, and often looked at an outsider as if I was a tropical fish. Often, it was too cold to even go outside. I looked at the map. Krissy's house was 777 miles from where I was, which felt mystical. It felt like a sign.

"I'll see you soon."

On March 29th I packed my car and headed south without a plan to return. I had no destination beyond Asheville. I was going there, maybe to stay for a while, and I didn't feel afraid. Maybe it was because the whole world was suddenly gripped in the terror and anxiety of hypochondria, and I had been training my whole life to live through a pandemic.

I drove straight through the Chicagoland morass, and this time it was easy. The road signs flashed "Go home." A late winter sky hung low and spat icy rain onto my windshield. All of Illinois and northern Indiana was gray and wet and cold. When I passed Indianapolis, I re-entered the world of color like a scene in Wizard of Oz. The grass was greener. People were out on golf courses. In Kentucky, the horses grazed in lush fields behind stands of vibrant cherry blossoms. Spring had come earlier here. The further I went, the brighter it got.

I got to Krissy's house right after sunset. The home sat on a high hill. Behind it, the city stretched into the distance toward the mountains. I took a photo because it was beautiful and just in case it could serve as evidence for the police investigating my disappearance. What I was doing felt insane. I was so used to transacting my way through the world in cold anonymity. I was used to paying people for an isolated space where I could be alone and therefore safe. This situation was demonstrably not alone, and therefore, my paranoid stray dog mind perceived it as potentially unsafe. On the road I languished in anonymity. It felt safe to be unknown. It meant I could disappear into the distance suddenly without anyone being disappointed. I had no one to answer to. But as the world shut down, the loneliness that had been churning inside came to a head and revealed a deep craving to be known. I wanted to be accountable to someone other than myself. I had traveled enough to get a sense of who I was, and to understand that I was ready for other people to get to know who I was, too. I craved community, consistency, and a place to root. I didn't know if people could be trusted, but I was beginning to understand that my lifestyle of beautiful, sterile isolation would not net out the growth and beauty that I wanted to create. This was my big swing.

Krissy answered the door, gave me a big hug, and welcomed me into a kitchen where dinner was on the stove. I sat on the floor and allowed myself to be mauled by their enormous shaggy dog, which put me instantly at ease, because you can tell a lot about someone by their dog. Mean dogs learn to be mean. Sweet, loving, open-hearted dogs don't happen by accident. With every enthusiastic lunge and lick, my trepidation diminished.

Presence

Staying still was richer than I imagined. Two weeks after landing in Asheville, I had my stuff pulled out of storage and delivered. I took things out of boxes that I had not seen since packing them in Denver three years prior. There was a sense of relief.

It was spring and flowers bloomed. Life was colorful and since the pandemic closed the civilized world it forced us outside. We hiked along the Blue Ridge Parkway and had picnics by the river. We went camping. We played board games and made homemade popcorn. We connected with other people who were making the most of the lockdowns, and a stream of new and interesting and unafraid people flooded into my life.

We built a microcosm of a community of people who bonded over creative projects and a mutual desire to feel connected in a world that wanted to separate us. Together, we brought creative projects to life. They encouraged me to write and cheered for each new story that I produced. Krissy let me help her bring a deck of animal-themed affirmation cards for kids into the world. While millions of people suffered through loneliness and isolation, we found a way to thrive through the insanity of a global pandemic by choosing to be together.

I stayed at Krissy's for almost eighteen months, re-learning to be a person who is known. It wasn't all easy. I got the 'rona and had to quarantine in an AirBnb a few towns over. Krissy and her husband tried unsuccessfully to get pregnant. I ached for autonomy and my own kitchen, and while I loved my room in their home, I felt ready to expand.

In August, almost a year and a half after arriving in Asheville, I started looking for a house of my own. I had heard purchasing a home in the hot market was impossible. People were trying for years and getting outbid even after offering thousands over the asking price. Houses were going for more than they could appraise for. There was a scarcity of high quality properties, and an influx of moneyed urbanites escaping the city for mellowness of the mountains. I had been dreamily scrolling homes on Zillow for a decade, noncommittally saving properties, keeping options open, feeling as though home ownership was out of reach not because of finances, but because of the overwhelming amount of options. How would I ever choose? If I was going to want this, and I was new to truly wanting things, I was going to need to focus. I needed to get clear on the exact details of the thing I wanted. I made a list.

I wanted an open kitchen and lots of natural light. I wanted the neighborhood to be set in nature, with lots of trees, and walkable. I identified two prime neighborhoods, both on the outskirts of town, convenient enough but removed. I wanted a big bathtub and a walk-in closet, and outdoor space. I wanted clean, but with character.

The day I began looking in earnest, after years of scrolling and dreaming through real estate listings, a little blue house on a mountain right down the road from that fateful yoga retreat dropped its price right into my budget. I called my realtor and, a few hours later, we were touring the bungalow with an open kitchen, high ceilings, and lots of natural light. It had a big tub and monster closet in the master. It was surrounded by forest and when the leaves fell promised to have a stunning view of the surrounding mountains.

We left and set out for the next house, a nearly identical home in a cabin style in the other neighborhood I loved. I walked in and thought *this isn't my house*—because I had already found mine. I felt it in my gut. I was calm, I was focused, I knew it was right. I put an offer in. They accepted. It all just fell perfectly into place. The inspections went well. All that was left was to close. Then, three days before closing, my mom died.

Things I Can't Outrun

These two boulder-sized milestones stacked on top of one another and then heaped on top of me. They were the kind of life moments that exhaust your emotional faculties so completely that you need a few weeks of alternating deep tissue massages and tear-soaked therapy sessions just to get back to baseline. And I got a twofer over one long weekend as Mom's passing punctuated my pinnacle with an unthinkable depth of sadness and stress. Her death was sudden, and it wasn't.

2021 was the final episode in a multi-year saga that left my powerful and vital mother a weak, unfocused, and sedentary shell. The illness was mysterious and deteriorative—diagnosed at various points as Lyme, leukemia, polymyalgia, and depression. Over a few short years, a woman who rose to corporate glory as a highly skilled HR executive could barely hold a conversation. Her sharp wit and strong opinions gave way to sluggishness. She was checked out and unmoved by most things, though her eyes lit up at the prospect of ice cream. She spent every single night entranced by the saccharine, formulaic love stories on the Hallmark channel. She became childlike.

Early on, it was weird and annoying. It was subtle enough that she may have just been leaning way too hard into retirement. All she wanted to do was relax. After decades of carrying our family on her back, that privilege was well-earned. As time went on and she slipped further into dullness, we panicked. We tried to re-engage her, get her up and fighting for the health and vitality she had hoped to achieve in her retirement. She was supposed to be living it up, but she just wanted to sit it out.

Her case confounded every doctor. Allopath nor naturopath could find anything wrong. Her blood work was fine. Never mind the pharmacy of prescriptions on the counter, never mind the fact that she spent her last few Halloweens in the hospital, suffering with vague and devastating symptoms. One year she was haunted by ghosts—falling hard, pulled downward by unseen forces. The next year she suffered a zombie affliction. I drove home through throngs of trick or treaters to find her where I left her days before, on the couch in her pajamas, conscious but unable to form a coherent sentence. Last year of course it was plague. She got hit by that famous respiratory illness. Despite cumulative weeks spent in hospitals, submitting to batteries of tests like a human lab rat, we always left with more prescriptions and fewer answers.

In January, unsure of what else to do, Dad planned a vacation. Sunshine would help, he figured. But she barely made it. She fell, like the first domino, down the escalator at the airport. She got up and said she was fine despite a bruised wrist and achy back and they made it to Florida where they discovered the fall had fractured a vertebra. She was put on bedrest to watch the waves crash from her hotel room. Dad found her unresponsive a few days later. An ambulance took her to the hospital, where she remained through Memorial Day. (Factually speaking, she bounced from one hospital to the next as Dad fought for higher quality of care, but for the sake of this narrative, it's only important that she was essentially medically imprisoned for four months.)

I went to visit her in a sparkling, multibillion-dollar high-rise hospital in Orlando. She was intubated and non-verbal, but her eyes sparkled when you talked to her. Her nurses were alert and engaged, chatting with her and keeping up with her vitals and getting her ready for more tests and procedures. They knew her name and her case. They let Dad hang out all day and graciously accepted his peace offerings of baked goods and snacks. Meanwhile, the doctors scooted around evasively on wheely laptop desks, avoiding our eyes and questions. They offered sparse detail, opting for monosyllabic explanations and lofty language. She seemed to be a series of numbers on a spreadsheet to them. It was the same every day. More data. Less clarity.

Dad and I went for a walk at the botanical gardens and vented our frustration. *If those motherfucking doctors gave a shit about her health, they'd bring her to a place like this where she could feel the sunshine on her face. They'd let her be outside and they'd feed her real food with some color in it. There was no way that fluorescent lights and beeping machines and fake brown sludge in her feeding tube were doing anything but making her sicker.*

Eventually she was discharged into a rehab center and then a nursing home and finally, some eighteen weeks after she fell at the airport, Dad arranged for a medical transport back home to Wisconsin. He had to pay for it out of pocket after fighting with insurance, because insurance was increasingly denying her claims because her case was not complex enough to cover. Her tracheotomy made her case too complex for most facilities in Wisconsin. So she landed at the only skilled nursing home that would take her, a prison-like structure on the bleakest street in Milwaukee.

She spent June and July there like some nightmare summer camp, marinating in the groaning and putrid smells of a ward otherwise populated with the vegetative. For her part, she got better. Dad brought her things from home, cards and flowers from friends, and ice cream from Culver's. People came to visit and filled her room with flowers and pictures from her days in the drum corps. Videos from her physical therapy sessions showed her almost standing up. Her voice got stronger, and we talked on the phone about the house I was buying and the man I was in love with. She sounded like herself as she expressed her excitement to get home. Dad was fighting to arrange in-home care. It seemed promising. There was light.

She made it home after almost eight months gone. Dad griped about adjusting to living with the caretaker, but finally felt some relief after so many fights with overworked nurses, belligerent doctors, uncaring insurance companies, and a nasty stress-induced skin infection. Mom's voice bubbled with joy—she was happy to be back in her home with her dog, looking out the windows to her big backyard.

A week later, she was gone.

Phone Calls

My phone rang at 5:09 on a Friday morning. Dad said, "Morning!" like it was normal, then he said, "Mom died." I remember because he spit the words out through his teeth, and they got lodged in my mind like an ax in a stump. Tersely, he said how it happened—something about blood oxygen. He said her tongue lolled out of her mouth, and that he kissed her and then she was gone. We were on the phone for three minutes and he hung up—the medical examiner was at the door—leaving me in shock in the dark.

My room was still and dark in the pre-dawn, and the world was silent beyond the blood pounding in my ears. I tried to pray. I clasped my hands and tried to sit still but couldn't. I was a buoy on an angry ocean, sloshing about on the surface. I didn't know what I was supposed to do. So I went outside, feeling the same impulse as a little kid who rushes outside on Christmas Eve to watch the sky for Santa's sleigh. Maybe I thought I could catch her on her way out. It wasn't Christmas, though, it was muggy and pitch black except for the misty halos from the streetlights. The sky over the mountains flashed in a late summer storm. I stood in the stillness and shook, shivering as mist clung to my skin.

In my restlessness, I got dressed and lit a candle with the Virgin Mary on it. Maybe I could light her way out a little. I stared at the flame but still couldn't sink in to pray although I wanted to. I craved some sense of connection, but my mind raced through shallow thoughts about driving home or catching a flight and what to do about the house closing on Monday. I felt conflicted. Do I continue with my ongoing commitments as if nothing happened, consult with the painters and let the cleaners in and work at the vintage pop-up over the weekend? Or do I shut everything down, cover my face with a veil and just moan for a week straight? It felt truly insane to do normal things like brush my teeth and make coffee, like the world was the same as it was yesterday. It wasn't. My mom was dead.

At 5:26, I called my boss.

After a decade of working together, I knew that Amy was the kind of weirdo that woke up at painful hours to get a jump start on her day. She answered because she is an angel. I told her what happened, pushing the words out through gravel in my throat. As I heard her gasp and express her first condolences, it finally sunk in. I wept. Amy listened, and asked me about my mom. She asked where she was from, if she had any siblings, how she met my dad, and what I admired about her. She asked what traits I inherited, and which were my favorite. I processed, reflected, and discovered things about my mom that I never realized. Amy and I talked for almost two hours. It was thousands of dollars' worth of therapy.

As the world woke up and the news spread, my phone began to light up. I spoke with a dozen people and had similar conversations. I accepted condolences and shared how I was feeling. The beginning of the conversations always hurt the most because we confronted the harsh reality of the situation. That's when my throat closes up and my heart pounds inside a metal cage. As the conversation goes on, I can rationalize and reframe and self-soothe until we're talking about how there is an odd comfort about grief, how I feel peace knowing that she's free from pain, and all the rest. I add those silver linings because I think that if I let them know I'm okay they'll feel better, too. By the time we're wrapping up I do feel better. Then the next person calls and I'm back at the beginning, back on the crest of the pain wave to begin processing once again.

Talking to her friends and family is nice, too. Hearing from people I haven't talked to in years reminds me of who she was before she got sick. At her peak, she was a queen.

She shone like a supernova in her career. She worked too much, traveled too much. It scared me and sometimes I resented her for choosing work over being home with us. Even while spending so much time on the road, she prioritized making her house a beautiful, comfortable shrine to return to. It was her sanctuary, and we got to live there too, and even cocreate it with her. Some Saturday mornings she would get a gleam in her eye and propose a redesign of some room in the house. We'd go get coffee at Borders (remember Borders?!) and thumb through the magazines for ideas. Then we'd set out to garage sales and HomeGoods to bring the vision to life. She had a great eye, and could bring a luxe magazine spread to life with stuff she found on clearance. We hunted and gathered until we were exhausted. Back at home, we'd throw a frozen pizza into the oven and put our changes into place while it cooked. The culminating moment was turning on the lamps, settling into comfy chairs, and burning our tongues on scorching pizza to admire our hard work.

So in my fairy dust optimism, I like to think that she left on purpose. She took her leave, knowing that I had a house to love and would be fine. She knew I would spend my weekends running errands like we used to. She knew that the house would give me endless distractions. After all the rushing about, though, there is the moment of sitting down, switching on the pretty lamp, and soaking it in. And that's when it caught up. When I sat still, I was pounded by the waves of emotion that I tried to outrun. If I didn't let myself feel it, I would just find myself weeping over a French press that warped and cracked in the move, heartbroken that coffee was leaking all over the counter and that I would never see my mom again.

The War on Grief

Grieving is different from what I expected, wider-reaching and insidious like a mycelium network of sadness. I expected to think of her in fond memories, to remember moments of sweet connection between us and be moved to graceful tears by the solemn knowing that we'd never share another. That happens sometimes—I cry when I think of the specifics like her handwriting or how her closet smelled. How she said the word 'Christmas' like a little kid because she loved the holiday that was so joyful, wholesome, and full of sweet things.

If I've gone too long without crying, I'll listen to old voicemails. She never said anything particularly profound or heartfelt, but I like to hear her voice.

"Hey Cakes, wondering when you'll be home so I can start the chicken. Call me back."

It occurs to me that voicemails won't degrade. They won't warp from use like the edges of a photograph held by tear-soaked fingers. We can't use the state of our digital media to measure the distance from grief, like when we saw pictures start to fade and crack. They will be perfect forever, even as the edges of our memories blur.

When I think of her legacy, I think of a great dinner party. She was warm and nourishing and brought people together. It's no surprise that she threw incredible get-togethers, from intimate dinners to Christmas open houses that attracted hundreds of guests. She planned them for weeks in advance, building thoughtful menus, laying in supplies, and recruiting us to prep the house. I set out crystal dishes of mixed nuts while she blasted the Doobie Brothers and taste-tested her cranberry wine sauce. There was a feeling of excitement that built to the climax of the first ring of the doorbell. When the guests left, and the CD changer reached the end of its rotation, and candle wax dripped on the tablecloth, the excitement gave way to calm accomplishment. She would sip a glass of scotch in the living room and reflect on the successful evening.

She used to tell me she wasn't creative, which always made me angry. Her homes and those parties were her art, and she was a master. I was her apprentice. Toward the end of her life, she stopped cooking. In the pie chart that represents my grieving emotions, between the slice of loss and the big hunk of grief, there is a portion of relief. It's another way that grieving is surprising, and shines light on feelings I didn't know were there.

If grieving was straightforward, I could just have a neat little mourning practice, but it's not. The sharpness of the first few days dissolved into sadness sludge that seeped into everything. Her death's blast left little emotional land-mines for me to stumble upon. My heart pounded when a phone rang. Rogue pains in my body invited me to fear the worst. I lashed out at loved ones and cried when people were mean in traffic. The resilience and confidence that she raised me to possess were out of reach while I mourned her. There was no bias-for-action in grieving, I just sat there and felt it.

The day she died, I worked at a bubbly vintage pop-up in downtown Asheville. I knew the tears would still be there after a few hours of distraction. I didn't tell anyone. I figured they would think I was insane. The truth is, I had been mourning the loss of my mother for years. That mystery ailment that attacked her nerves and locked her mind in a cage stole her from me. She was checked out, unresponsive, uninterested. Her eyes were glazed over. The woman I knew already left. That life was already over. Now we were simply mourning the loss of her physical form. There is comfort in the inevitability of death. In a world where everything feels so uncertain most of the time, it's nice to know there's at least one thing we can count on.

There is peace knowing that she's free from the body that imprisoned her. There is relief knowing she died at home, where she was happy. I picture God tapping her on the shoulder and asking if she is ready to go, and her eyes lit up and she went because she knew everyone that she was here to care for was going to be fine. I feel a sense of freedom for her, next to the deep grief of realizing that she won't see me get married, won't see my house, won't meet my kids.

Behind all the shallow rationalizations and comforting feelings of relief, there is still a chasm of deep loss. All I need to do is remember my dad's words—"Mom died"—and I feel the hole that she left. She birthed me and raised me to be strong. She gave me priceless gifts like business sense and a built-in abundance mindset. I got her textured hair and champagne taste.

She put five separate people through college. That's one of my favorite facts about her, and why we're exploring the idea of setting up a scholarship in her name. It's fitting for the woman who dedicated her life to helping others succeed. She cared deeply about potential and expressed very little patience when it went unrealized. Being raised by someone with such high standards was a very mixed blessing. I did not have the option to bring home a mediocre report card, because she knew that I was capable of better. To pull anything less than straight A's was to betray her understanding of my abilities, and it simply would not do. She instilled an attitude of excellence and achievement in me. It was never questioned that I would go to and graduate college and follow in her footsteps with a "good" job. It was a foregone conclusion that I would follow her path and do so with some degree of success. It was our family business.

We hosted the after-party for her memorial service at the sprawling house she bought with the specific intent to entertain her family and friends in her retirement. In her absence, everyone looked to me for answers, as if I had ascended her throne. I was woefully unprepared. She had decades of experience entertaining and knew how many napkins to set out and how much ice to buy. These things I used to think were trivial, now that I had to answer to the hungry, I understood. Her legacy was about tasteful entertaining, and it was about service, community, family, booming laughter, great food, and spreading the warmth of time well-spent. I will remember her parties like the final scenes of a Hallmark movie. While snow falls gently outside, a happy family gathers in a gently-lit Christmas scene and two lovers share a kiss under the mistletoe while a golden retriever puppy snoozes by the fire.

Several Fridays passed. The house came together nicely, thanks to many days of manic rushing about, gathering items like end tables and dish towels. I still worked myself into a frothy mania trying to outrun the grief that sat like a concrete slab in my heart. When I turned onto my new road toward my new house, the thought still occurred to me to call her. So, I would. I'd take a deep breath and say "Hi, Mom," and we would talk for a while.

Her life—and her death—show that I can run all I'd like. I can climb the corporate ladder, chase that golden ring, move a hundred times. Life will still catch up. That gotta-go mentality ultimately destroyed her. If I'm not mindful, it can catch up with me, too. By embodying the opposite, she taught me to stop and rest before life forces my hand. She died to teach us not to save it for the end, because the end might not wait for you to be ready. In her honor, I will raise a glass (scotch for her, spring water for me) and drink in the moment.

Becoming HALF WILD

I survived. I'm actually doing really well, thanks, kind of like my whole life was preparing for this. I needed to heal—hard—to be ready for the impending chaos of a world where I am put through a spin cycle of highs and lows. I needed to feel the deep discomfort of betraying myself through bad habits that I knew were not mine. I had to inquire and discover those mechanisms that drove me to numb out, and I had to step tenderly back into the intensity of presence. It took time, as everything worthwhile does. It took tectonic shifts of mindset that informed the glacial pace of habit changes, and it took repeated, intentional moments of recognition. *Holy shit, I'm doing it.*

A podcast about oxalates helped me fix my joint pain.

An acupuncturist suggested I quit dairy, a change which, when stacked on top of a thousand other changes, basically destroyed my anxiety. The chest tightness, fluttering heart, and hypoglycemic spikes that triggered my hypochondriac panic attacks all subsided when I removed cheese as a food group. On top of learning how to breathe with Maureen, discovering I could be there for the scared little girl inside me that still wondered what lurked in the dark, and getting in uncompromising touch with my body meant that I could finally hear the signals my body wanted to send.

I could discern, determine, and move forward boldly, still informed by the years of experience, missteps, and fuckups. That confluence of factors is what comes together in HALF WILD.

What does it mean to be HALF WILD?

HALF WILD means wearing cashmere in the wilderness.

It's showing up with everything you've learned, then leaving it all behind because you finally understand that you've always had everything you needed within, the whole time. Like Dorothy and her ruby slippers, you had the power inside you all along.

It's not needing anything, really. It's taking comfort in the fact that you can provide for yourself, you can fill your void with breath and forgiveness, and when you come out of that zen state you can still have desires, and you can love the things you want. Living HALF WILD, I showed up to vegetarian yoga retreats with a suitcase full of beef jerky, firm in the understanding of what my body really needs. It means understanding that our basest animal emotions are powerful signals toward growing toward the divine.

It's recognizing how we are the creators of everything that haunts us, we are complicit in our pain, and feeling empowered by the understanding that we get to co-create how we experience it. If we can get stuck in crappy feeling habits, we can also get 'stuck' in habits that facilitate contentment and expansion. We can flow with life like leaves on the stream instead of trying to steer the river.

HALF WILD is the recognition that it's okay to crave beauty and wildness and order and destruction. It's okay to be exactly where we are, and okay to want to burn everything to the ground and start over. It's about trusting that the best guidance is often louder and closer and scarier than the so-called experts. It's an invitation to end the habit of outsourcing everything to others and taking radical responsibility for how we show up, getting painfully real with how we limit ourselves through self-delusion and excuses.

HALF WILD means discovering what's destroying you, and being brave enough to understand the call might be coming from inside the house. Your agony may be an inside job. For decades a voice within howled for my attention and I ignored it because it scared me. When I was brave enough to reframe it and listen, I discovered a scared little girl who just wanted to be held, and that I could hold her and all of her fears and confusion about who she was supposed to be in this world. I could comfort her and quiet the raging discomfort of being alive in an uncertain world. I can even let her howl run the show.

It's hearing, absorbing, and integrating that our limiting beliefs are often lies, and breaking the cycle of analysis paralysis perfectionism based on the belief that the things you want are out of reach unless you kill yourself for them. It's letting go of the slimy comfort of "not enough."

HALF WILD is trusting the flow, stepping away from overthinking and overplanning and perfection in favor of gentle nudges toward alignment. It's giving up on the mirage of "most best" and embracing the real feeling of the "right now." I stopped working so hard, recognizing that the paradigm of virtue in struggle was outdated and needlessly exhausting. It's dismantling the ego that says that everything worth doing must be done hard. Anything worth getting takes a decade and a truckload of elbow grease. If it's not painful, strenuous, arduous, well, you're doing it wrong.

It's feeling safely at home in your wild body and wild emotions. It's feeling it all through the inevitable storms of life. It's taking comfort in knowing that life will happen, things will change, loved ones will leave, and you'll feel it all and be stronger for it, unless it makes you softer, which is okay too. It's about having your feet in the mud but good shoes nearby, feeling it all, taking it in, sniffing the wind, and hearing a call from deep within that says *let's go for it.*

It's embracing change and nurturing green shoots of love sprouting from the fertile soil of a once-barren heart, protected under lock and key for fear that someone might ruin it. It's recognizing that holding back isn't protective, it's just ruining it yourself. It's breaking from cycles of distraction and playing small to let dreams come into focus. I always assumed my dream would knock on my door like the Publisher's Clearing House with a giant check and my life would shift into the "dream life." But no, dreams emerge slowly. Life changes so slowly you barely notice—until one morning you wake up healthy and happy and in love and at home.

It wasn't about growing up. It is about growing in.

* * *

ACKNOWLEDGMENTS

In acknowledgment of some of the helpers, space-holders, and wayshowers who helped birth these stories into being:

I would not have been brave enough to write this book and get it across the finish line if not for the incredibly strong, supportive, and whip smart women in my life who, in their unflinching faith, helped me recognize my capacity to create. If these high priestesses believe in me, I must be on to something. Thank you Amy, Amanda, Davida, and Patricia. You are diamonds in a gravel path.

Shout out to my parents for always talking to me like a grown-up. You cultivated my wild mind when you encouraged me to read, both directly and by being voracious readers yourselves. Thanks for Scrabble nights, naming-and-rhyming on so many long road trips, and for nurturing my imagination with freedom and a safe place to land.

Thank you Katie for re-invigorating my love of writing and reminding me who I have always been. Your joyful, encouraging, and teacherly ways helped me bring *Brave Girls* to life and I finally had something I was proud of that I wanted to build on. Of course it was you. And if it wasn't you, then it was Ewan MacGregor, and I dreamed it.

Thanks to Virginia and Maureen for refusing to believe my excuses and pushing me to be more honest and present with myself; for a thousand arched eyebrows and challenges to do better and see clearer, and for being my cheerleaders when I finally could.

Thank you Krissy, you bright-eyed guiding light. You were the first to plant the seed that my stories could be a book, and the creative vortex we created in 2020 was unreal. I will forever cherish Story Nights with you, Ev, Mowgli, and the bears.

Thank you Marco, for loving me enough to tell me to "shut up and write." You're a catalyst and an expert at calling out BS and resistance tactics. I'm unspeakably grateful that you walked into my life and made all the hard parts easier. You are my home.

Thanks to Abigail who also wandered into my house by no accident at all. The cosmic tumblers aligned to bring us together so we could bring beautiful things to life. I am endlessly thankful for your acumen, clarity, and guidance. You're making it all real.

Finally, thanks to my classmates at San Ramon Valley High who read my snarky columns in *The Wolfprint* and named me Most Likely to Write a Best-Selling Autobiography in the yearbook Senior Superlatives. Let's see if you were right about me after all.

-Whitney

ABOUT THE AUTHOR

Inspired by mythology and wanderlust, Whitney spent her early life traveling in search of a place that felt like home. Her adventures continued to lead her further from her true residence, which she ultimately found in a small, beating space within her chest. She writes to make sense of a complex world and to function as a channel for the muse, who loves it when she lets her eyes roll back in her head and her fingers dance wildly across the keyboard.

Whitney graduated with a degree in Comparative Literature from the University of Colorado, where she put on a masterclass in procrastination and binge drinking. She currently works remotely as a strategic content manager for a technology startup accelerator where she builds storytelling frameworks for entrepreneurs. She loves to systemize, and will someday apply that skill to her personal blog and newsletter, published under the HALF WILD name at halfwilddispatches.com.

Whitney loves dogs, dinner parties, and talking to strangers. Her love of nature, lush greenery, and gentle competition compel her to the golf course or the hiking trail as often as possible. She is passionate about exploring ways to eat, live, love, and travel well. She is happily settled—for the moment—in the mountains of Asheville, North Carolina.